HIDING MY UNHAPPINESS: THE PLAY

TABLE OF CONTENTS

HIDING MY UNHAPPINESS

CHARACTERS:

JANICE JONES	HUMAN RESOURCE SPECIALIST
DE'ANDRE JONES	CPA – JANICE HUSBAND
FELICIA WILLIAMS	HAIR STYLIST – JANICE CHILDHOOD FRIEND
YOLANDA JONES	JANICE DAUGHTER
BELINDA JONES	JANICE DAUGHTER
TIANNA ROBERTSON	DENTIST – JANICE CHILDHOOD FRIEND
MIGUEL JONES	DE'ANDRE BROTHER
SYERRA JONES	FITNESS INSTRUCTOR – DE'ANDRE SISTER
MYESHA FERGUSON	REGISTERED NURSE – JANICE SISTER
JERMAINE GRISBY	JANICE CO-WORKER
MALAYSHA WILSON	JANICE CO-WORKER
CAMERON TUCKER	RESTAURANT OWNER
SHERISE PALMER	JANICE CO-WORKER
DANIELLE THOMAS	CLINICAL THERAPIST – JANICE COUSIN
KANDACE FINCH	TAX AUDITOR – DE'ANDRE CO-WORKER
CARMEN PRICE	ENTREPRENUER – JANICE COUSIN
MILDRED FERGUSON	JANICE GRANDMOTHER
DOMINIC FERGUSON	JANICE BROTHER
RHONDA FERGUSON	JANICE SISTER
LACHELLE MITCHELL	JANICE COUSIN
CHERYL WALLACE	MARRIAGE COUNSELOR

This play is based on true event that happens in people's lives in one way or another. Even though that all the characters in the storyline are fiction, some of the events are as realistic as you would see it. We all have had some family members that are going through trials and tribulations in which they feel that it is either no end or no hope no matter what they try. We have seen situations where we have people in our lives that we think have our best interest and at the end of the day, we get disappointed by those that we thought so highly of. It is just a vicious cycle of betrayal that we not only ever expected, but we have given our all to people we call our loved ones. We find ourselves getting hurt and losing trust of one another. In some cases, there is jealousy that is in existence. There are those closes to you that either wants what you have or does not want you to have what you have. At that point, unconditional love is out the window. This career-oriented woman must take control of her life and make sure that her priorities are in order. She will find out that when her priorities are all over the place, she stresses herself so bad that she becomes an emotional wreck. With the struggles that she is having in her family, she is on the verge of losing everything at all cost. Her marriage becomes extremely rocky. She seeks counseling to help put the pieces of the puzzle back in place where it needs to be. In the midst of her ordeal, by her thinking about making everyone else happy, she was making herself unhappy.

SCENE 1 – CONVERSATIONS WITH YOUR DAILY ENVIRONMENT:

Janice:

Man, I knew that I was coming into a lot of work this Monday morning. With all that we have to catch up on, it seems like my whole week is pretty much planned.

Jermaine:

Good morning Janice, how was your weekend?

Janice:

Good morning Jermaine. My weekend was great. I was very busy but it was great. How was yours?

Jermaine:

It went to quick. Didn't get everything done that I was trying to accomplish.

Malaysha:

Hey Jermaine, Hey Janice.

Janice:

Hey Malaysha. Girl, I like that outfit.

Jermaine:

Hey Babygirl.

Malaysha:

Thank you Janice. I caught it on sale this weekend at the mall. It was a good thing that I didn't have more money or I would still be there.

Jermaine:

It is a good thing that you are single because you would have destroyed a man's credit card. I know if I was your man, I would have already filed bankrupt for the second time.

Malaysha:

(Chuckles) Boy, you are crazy. I am not that bad. If I had a man, I wouldn't be spending like crazy.

Jermaine:

That is easier said than done. With you having the freedom to do what you want when you want for as long as you have been doing it, you don't just turn it off

Malaysha:

It is easy for me because I understand the concept of responsibility. I am taking every moment to enjoy the fruits of my labor. I make sure my bills are paid first. All I have are household responsibilities. No loans or credit cards all at.

Janice:

That is good. I wish I could say that. I have debt that seems like I would never get out of.

Malaysha:

Janice, what is going on with you? Why so much debt if you don't mind me asking?

Janice:

I was helping my family. They needed my help and I didn't want to leave them hanging.

Jermaine:

Janice, you better stop that because in the end you will always be at a lost when it comes to finances. Trust me, you do not want to go down that road.

Malaysha:

Janice, Jermaine is right. You have to tell your family no because if you don't, they will drain you dry and think nothing of it. Trust me, I had family that tried doing the same thing with me. They even tried the guilt trip concept on me. It worked for a little bit but after it was all said and done, I was disappointed because there were things that I wanted to do but couldn't. I said never again will I deprive myself.

Janice:

I understand what you are saying Malaysha. I hate seeing my family in need. They be needing my help.

Malaysha:

Girl, believe me. It is not the help that they need. It is the opportunity that you give them to take advantage of you. I'm telling you as a real friend that it is not good. It is like you are working for them and letting them cash your paycheck. I got one question. What does your husband say?

Janice:

There is a lot that he doesn't know.

Malaysha:

Girl, are you crazy? Do you know how mad he would be?

Janice:

I know. I can't tell him. He may end up leaving me. He was so mad one time that I was helping my cousin. He did not talk to me for a week.

Sherise:

Good morning everyone. I tell you that my day has already started off rough. First, the six-car pileup slowed us down and I lost an hour stuck in traffic. Other than that, how was everyone's weekend?

Jermaine:

Mine was great.

Malaysha:

I can't complain. It went quick.

Janice:

Ok. I was extremely busy helping family.

Sherise:

Helping family? Please tell me that you are talking about your husband and your two daughters?

Malaysha:

No Sherise. She is helping her extended family. I told her that her husband and her daughters are her family.

Sherise:

Janice, what does your husband think or do he know? I hope that you are not still giving money to them.

Janice:

You all don't understand. They need my help. My husband does not know. He would be extremely mad if he did.

Sherise:

He would have every right to be upset. You are going to mess around and lose a good man behind some nonsense.

Janice:

You think he would leave me? I cook, clean and make sure that the house is straight.

Sherise:

That is fine and all but you are taking care of something that is not your responsibility. On top of that, you are keeping secrets from him.

Malaysha:

Janice, she is telling the truth. You are not helping. You are giving to some that don't want to do anything to make a living. They figure as long as they got you, they don't have to do anything. I know you give to quite a few in the family. I bet you give more to the ones that I see calling and bugging you the most. Your brother Dominic and your cousin Lachelle are the two main individuals that is always blowing up your phone.

Janice:

Lachelle has five kids and she is doing it by herself. I'm helping Dominic catch up on his child support so they don't lock him up. My sister Rhonda no so much. I have no clue what she does but she always has money.

Sherise:

Janice, stop enabling them. Both situations have to do with kids. Both situations are kids that are not your responsibility. Janice, if your husband finds out, you are going to have problems. Trust me, I lost mine.

Janice:

Oh really. You and your husband are not together?

Sherise:

He left me about three years ago. I didn't understand until some family members of mine opened my eyes telling me losing him was my fault. They told me that I didn't take care of him like I took care of other family members that I don't talk to at all anymore. I defended them when he was trying to tell me that they do not have your best interest. He really was a good man. We were married seven years. Now my true love is gone.

Malaysha:

I never been married but I lost out on a great opportunity. There was a guy that my cousin convinced me that he was no good. Being naive, I listened to her. Two years later, my cousin ended up getting with him and she married him.

Janice:

Do you ever look back and think how your life would have been like if you would have not listened to her and followed your heart?

Malaysha:

I think about it all the time. Don't get me wrong, I am good being single. It is nice to have the companionship when you want someone to hug and hold you.

Sherise:

Janice, what Malaysha is saying is the God's honest truth. You have that right at home. Please do not blow it. I don't know what you have going on in your personal life, but do not allow any distractions. That will definitely drive a wedge between what you have.

Janice:

I understand what you all are saying. It is just very hard knowing that my family needs help. I just feel guilty knowing that I could have prevented them from getting into a bind. I know that you are right about my husband. I will make sure that I get things right.

Jermaine:

Speaking from a man's point of view, once we feel like something is not right, we will press an issue. The minute we have an issue, for the most part we want it solved to alleviate the drama. There are not too many men that likes dealing with drama. Not saying there are absolutely none, just saying not too many.

Janice:

I know that my husband hates drama. Anytime he feels drama is present, he will immediately separate himself from it. He is the type "Let people hand their own business". If it doesn't involve us, let's stay in our own lane.

Sherise:

Janice, you have to always put family first. You also need some time away from family members and focus on yourself.

Malaysha:

I think we all need to take a girl's trip for Janice so she can clear her head.

Janice:

What do you have in mind?

Malaysha:

Me, you, Sherise and your daughters.

Sherise:

I am definitely overdue for a getaway.

Malaysha:

I have a friend that is a travel agent. I will give her a call later on to see if there are any specials out there.

Janice:

That will work for me. I know that my daughters will enjoy that. We can probably plan for either spring break or summer. Either one will do because the girls will be out of school then.

Malaysha:

What year are they in?

Janice:

Yolanda is a senior in college pursuing medical school afterwards. Belinda is a sophomore in college pursing to be an architect.

Malaysha:

OMG, that is outstanding.

Janice:

They are also heavily involved in the community. Yolanda is an AKA and Belinda is a Delta. It is like they are kind of following their father's footsteps. De'Andre is an Omega.

Sherise:

All those divine nine in one house. You didn't pledge?

Janice:

No I didn't. No reason in particular.

Sherise:

That is great. Husband is a CPA, plus you two are parents of a future doctor and architect.

Janice:

I am proud of both of them.

Malaysha:

Man, I am hungry. What are we getting for lunch?

Sherise:

Let's order from Cameron's restaurant. They serve some good food. He serves a variety of food. I went there for dinner one day. A friend of mines told me to try something from the soul food list.

Jermaine:

Cameron's restaurant it is. Everyone write down what you want so I can call it in.

Janice:

Here is the list with everyone's order. Make sure we get plenty of napkins.

Jermaine:

Ok, I am getting ready to place the order.

Malaysha:

I will finish this quarterly report after I eat because my stomach is growling.

Sherise:

I know what you mean. I ate a small breakfast this morning and I am starving.

Jermaine:

They will be here in about thirty minutes.

Sherise:

While we are waiting on our food, lets discuss where should we go for a girl's trip. I have a couple of ideas.

Malaysha:

I called my travel agent friend when I took my fifteen-minute break. She said come up with a place of destination and she will put a package plan together.

Janice:

I was thinking about three places. Myrtle Beach, Pigeon Forge and Punta Canta are the three of my choice.

Sherise:

Punta Canta sounds nice. The other two I thought about was Cabo Mexico and the Caribbean.

Malaysha:

For me, the Bahamas and any of the others that yall already said.

Jermaine:

Hey everyone, the food has arrived.

Cameron:

Good afternoon everyone.

Janice:

Hey Cameron. Long time no see.

Cameron:

I know right. It has been since high school. How is your family?

Janice:

Everyone is doing fantastic. We are going to getting together soon to celebrate my mother's birthday. We are bringing her to your restaurant.

Cameron:

Ok cool. Make sure that you let me know when it takes place so I can have something set up for her. Please tell your mom that I said hello. You all take care. I have a couple of more deliveries.

Janice:

Take care. Nice to see you again.

Malaysha, Sherise, Jermaine:

Take care.

Malaysha:

Is he married or is he single? I would mind being his queen. He is a hustler and got his own business. He is definitely a keeper.

Janice:

He was married. Been divorced for about five years now. A couple of our high school classmates get together often. I spoke to my friend Tianna at my last dentist visit. She was telling me that he is one of her patients. We were talking about our classmates and what they are doing of the classmates that is still local. She said she frequents his restaurant once every two weeks.

Malaysha:

I take it that she talks to him often?

Janice:

I can say that it is safe to say she speaks with him often.

Sherise:

Did we determine where we were going? I would say Myrtle Beach because of the cost and for us to have more money to spend unless Malaysha's friend has a great deal for us.

Malaysha:

I sent her all the information with the number of people and the number of days to be gone.

Janice:

I'm looking forward to it. This is long overdue.

Sherise:

Yes it is. I am definitely looking forward to this.

Jermaine:

I guess when you all are going on the trip, I will have the office to myself (chuckles).

Malaysha:

Yes, you will be in charge when we are gone (chuckles). We have about two hours left before we head home for the day. I am about to knock out this quarterly report.

Janice:

I just submitted my reports to the audit department. Once they do their part and send it back to me, I can record it and file it away.

Sherise:

All of mine is complete. About to finish the rest of my food that I didn't finish earlier.

Malaysha:

My friend just emailed me the packages and the cost for the trip. I am opening the email now. It looks like Myrtle Beach is cheaper. The other places are much more expensive. The advantage to Myrtle Beach for me is that I have family not too far if we want some country home cooking while we are in the area.

Sherise:

I am for that.

Janice:

I'm in. Myrtle Beach it is.

Jermaine:

It is about that time to get out of here for today.

Malaysha:

Janice, remember what we talked about. Think about yourself and your family. That is more important. Everyone you are helping are grown. Again, the key word is grown.

Sherise:

That is such a true statement Janice. Think about you first and what you are responsible for.

Janice:

I hear you all. I promise that I will work more on me before even thinking about anyone else.

<u>Sherise:</u>

Ok now. We are going to hold you to that. But as always, we are here if you ever need to talk. We will be here with an open mind and a listening ear.

<u>Jermaine:</u>

Ok everyone, let's get out of here. I see you all tomorrow.

<u>Sherise:</u>

Take care, see you tomorrow Janice and Malaysha.

<u>Malaysha:</u>

Bye everyone.

<u>Janice:</u>

See you all tomorrow.

<u>END OF SCENE 1</u>

SCENE 2 – JANICE ARRIVES HOME AFTER RUNNING ERRANDS:

Janice:

Hello!!! Is anyone home?

Yolanda:

Mom, we are upstairs.

Belinda:

Hey mom, how was your day?

Janice:

Work is work. Extremely blessed to have a job. Has anyone of you talked to your dad? I thought that he would have been home by now.

Yolanda:

I spoke with him earlier to see how his day was going. He said that he was extremely busy.

Belinda:

I hadn't talked to him.

Janice:

I tried calling him twice but couldn't get him.

Yolanda:

What time did you try calling? I know when I caught him, he had just finished a conference. He and his co-worker Kandace grabbed something quickly to eat before going back into their conference.

Janice:

Oh really!!!

Belinda:

Mom, don't do that. Don't get to thinking negatively. You know he is a workaholic.

Yolanda:

You know that his ultimate goal is to own his own accounting firm one day. He is ready to leave that firm like yesterday.

Janice:

I know what you two are saying. My mind is just all over the place. By the way, me and the girls at work were talking about a girl's trip we are planning. Of course, you two are included in the girl's trip.

Yolanda & Belinda:

Really, where are we going?

Janice:

Looks like it will be Myrtle Beach. Every other place we were looking were expensive. We are looking at either going during spring break or summer break.

Yolanda:

I am good with either one.

Belinda:

Me too.

"THE DOOR BELL RINGS"

Yolanda:

Mom, it is uncle Dominic.

<u>Janice:</u>

What in the world do he want? Let him in.

<u>Dominic:</u>

Hey everyone.

<u>Janice:</u>

Dominic, what are you doing here?

<u>Dominic:</u>

Is this the way that you talk to your loving brother big sis?

<u>Janice:</u>

Don't play with me. Every time I see you, it is always leading to needing money. I am going to let you know now that I do not have any money.

<u>Dominic:</u>

Come on sis. All I need is something to hold to carry me through the rest of the month. I am trying to get the system off of my back. They are trying to lock me up again. How do they expect me to take care of my responsibilities if they keep locking me up?

<u>Janice:</u>

Dominic, you need to hold a job longer than a week in order for them to take you seriously and leave you alone. You do not take life serious at all. You have responsibilities that you need to take care of. You are my brother but I know that you have been slacking. You already know better so I shouldn't even be having this conversation with you.

<u>Dominic:</u>

Sis, I didn't come for the long lecture. You know that I am trying but things are hard for me right now. Are you going to help me or what?

Janice:

Dominic, why are you raising your voice?

Dominic:

Sis, I am sorry. If you help me, I can get out of your hair. Come on sis so I can make some moves.

Janice:

Here Dominic. Now get out before my husband get home.

Dominic:

Thanks sis. Bye everyone.

Yolanda:

Mom, why do you keep supporting his habits? Mom, you know that he is a sorry man. He doesn't take care of none of his kids.

Belinda:

Mom, most of the time that I see him, he is getting something to drink. Mom, you cannot keep doing this.

Yolanda:

Belinda, now that you say that, he was with some guys I knew hanging around in an area crawling with trouble. Most of them hang out at Jackie's corner store.

Janice:

Your uncle said that he was trying to change his life and be in all his kid's life.

<u>Belinda:</u>

I will believe it when I see it. I think his oldest child is either eight or nine years old. I ran into the mother at the store and she told me to let uncle Dominic know that she needed help getting her daughter clothes since she has outgrown everything. She said uncle Dominic has done nothing at all since the baby was born. She did mention about some clothes that she knew you bought for her. She told me to tell you thank you.

<u>Janice:</u>

The baby needed some clothes and I didn't want her wearing clothes that didn't fit.

<u>Yolanda:</u>

Mom, what is it going to take to get you to stop? It is not your responsibility.

<u>Belinda:</u>

Mom, you need to cut your brother loose to contributing to his responsibilities. You cannot keep doing this.

"GARAGE DOOR IS OPENING"

<u>Janice:</u>

That is your dad pulling up. He cannot know about this. We have been getting along and I don't want to spoil it. Please keep this between us.

<u>Yolanda:</u>

It is not fair to him. You need to stop.

<u>Janice:</u>

We will talk about it later.

"DOOR FROM THE GARAGE OPENS"

De'Andre:

Hello Babe, how are you? How was your day?

Janice:

It was great sweetheart.

De'Andre:

Hey Yolanda & Belinda. How are my favorite girls doing?

Yolanda & Belinda:

We are good. How about you?

De'Andre:

I will be better once I get a hug.

Janice:

What do you want for dinner?

De'Andre:

We can order pizza if you want since it is a little late to cook.

Janice:

Why are you so late getting off of work?

De'Andre:

End of the quarter audits and reports we have to do for all the companies that we contract with. You know we do quarterly reports every March, June, September and December. This is nothing new to you.

Janice:

Why did it take so long? Didn't you have any help?

De'Andre:

There was a team of us doing this plus the various conferences we had.

Janice:

Was Kandace part of the team?

De'Andre:

She works in the firm with us. Yes, she is a part of the team. What is it about Kandace? You specifically ask about her even though we have other women and interns there.

Janice:

I was just asking.

De'Andre:

Look, don't start with that. This isn't the first time you inquired about her and it probably won't be the last time. I am going to take a shower.

"DE'ANDRE LEAVES THE ROOM TO TAKE A SHOWER"

Yolanda:

Mom, why are you interrogating dad about Kandace? Kandace is like an aunt to us. I thought you two were cool?

Janice:

I don't have anything against her at all. It is just that your dad is always talking about how much of a team player she is. I only hear about her but no other females.

Belinda:

You have to think about it. They been working together for over fifteen years. She has the experience that others probably don't have.

Janice:

I know he wants to start his own firm and want to bring her on board with him.

Yolanda:

What will the problem be if she will be a major contribution to the business? Wouldn't you want his business to be successful?

Janice:

Of course, I would.

Belinda:

Ok then mom, what is the real problem?

Janice:

Your dad is done with his shower. We will talk later.

De'Andre:

Has the pizza arrived yet?

Janice:

We haven't ordered it yet.

De'Andre:

What are we waiting on?

Janice:

We were waiting on you to get out of the shower to see exactly what you want.

De'Andre:

Janice, you know what I always get.

Janice:

Belinda, go ahead and place the order.

De'Andre:

Janice, what is going on with you?

Janice:

Nothing, I am just tired.

De'Andre:

You seem like you are in a crappy mood. You act like something is bothering you. Whatever it is, you need to come out with it.

Janice:

You think something is bothering me?

De'Andre:

You ask me about work like you think I am up to something. Afterwards, you start questioning me about Kandace. So yes, I think something is bothering you.

Janice:

Like I said, nothing is bothering me.

De'Andre:

Ok. I am going to leave it alone. I know otherwise, but if you choose to say nothing then there is nothing to bring up later.

Janice:

Now, what is that suppose to mean?

De'Andre:

You know exactly what I mean. One minute, you are feeling one type of way and the next, you feel another type of way. Your wishy-washy ways are becoming annoying. You are even grouchy when I leave out in the morning. I know that I haven't done anything to you. Whoever you are mad at, you need to square that away.

"THE DOOR BELL RINGS"

Yolanda:

I'll get it. It is the pizza delivery person.

Janice:

Here is the money plus their tip.

Belinda:

I am definitely ready to eat.

Yolanda:

Everything smells good. dad, the food is here.

De'Andre:

Janice, we will talk later.

Yolanda:

Belinda, you were not playing around. You were definitely hungry from the looks of your plate.

Belinda:

True that. dad, you don't have much on your plate.

De'Andre:

Not that hungry. I have to run and catch your uncle Miguel before he goes to bed. I am going to pick up some money he has for me.

Janice:

That can't wait until tomorrow?

De'Andre:

No because he is leaving tomorrow for a couple of days.

Janice:

So, you necessarily need it tomorrow? It can't wait until he gets back?

De'Andre:

You can go with me if you want.

Janice:

No. Go ahead.

"DE'ANDRE LEAVES OUT"

Yolanda:

Now mom, was that even necessary? Let's continue with our earlier conversation. Something is on your mind.

Belinda:

Mom, I have to agree with Yolanda. Do you think dad has a thing for Kandace? I say that because of all the questions.

Janice:

I don't know. I mean look at Kandace. She is gorgeous. I know that should not mean anything but sometimes I think in the back of my mind, I wonder if he is attracted to her. She is single, make good money and can have any guy that she wants.

Yolanda:

Has dad ever given you a reason to think he is interested in her?

Janice:

I can't say he has. It bugs me a little knowing that there is a gorgeous woman with him all through the day.

Yolanda:

Should that matter because they are in the same profession?

Janice:

No, not at all.

Belinda:

Mom, if he hasn't given you a reason to thinking otherwise, don't add to a problem that doesn't exist. Contributing to stress that may already be there can push any person to find some comfort anywhere. You will be making it easy.

Yolanda:

Have you ever tried telling him how you feel or do you approach him indirectly without an open mind?

Janice:

I never really told him how I feel without emotionally blowing up at him. I have the intentions on talking with him but once my emotions get in the way, all kind of thoughts start flying.

Belinda:

Has it ever occurred to you that he would probably distance himself because he has no idea what is going on? Has he tried talking to you and you shut him down? You have to take those things into consideration.

"GARAGE DOOR IS OPENING"

Janice:

I hear the garage door opening. Your dad is back. I will truly work on what two were saying. It just takes me a little time.

Yolanda:

Try not to take too long. Time is valuable.

De'Andre:

I'm back.

Yolanda:

Hey there. I am about to call it a night.

Belinda:

I am right there with you. Good night mom and dad?

Janice & De'Andre:

Good night you two.

De'Andre:

Now are you ready to talk?

Janice:

Yes I am. Where did we leave off at?

De'Andre:

Let's start off with what is bothering you and what is on your mind because have been tripping lately.

Janice:

At times, I think you spend a lot of your time at work. Sometimes I do not feel that I have your undivided attention.

De'Andre:

What do you consider a lot of time at work? If you ever think about owning a business, it takes a lot of time and you know it. You know I plan on having my own firm. You said that you don't have my undivided attention. Ninety percent of the time when I come in, you are on the phone. How do you expect to have my undivided attention?

Janice:

I just think that you could make more time for me.

De'Andre:

We both work basically the same hours and home at the same time. I don't understand when you say I don't make time. We are here. You never want to do anything.

Janice:

You never asked.

De'Andre:

You are the one who brought it up about never making time. You do not know what you want.

Janice:

It seems like work is more important.

De'Andre:

It is a reason that you are saying that. When you decide to tell me what it is, then maybe it will make you feel better. You are speaking in riddles and dancing around whatever issue you have.

<u>Janice:</u>

Don't worry about it. I'm getting tired. Got to get up early tomorrow.

<u>De'Andre:</u>

Not worried at all. Maybe later or maybe not.

"DE'ANDRE AND JANICE TURNS IN FOR THE NIGHT"

<u>END OF SCENE 2</u>

SCENE 3 – A NEW DAY WITH SOME NEW PERSPECTIVES:

Yolanda:

Good morning everyone. I made breakfast.

De'Andre:

Thank you Babygirl. I am going to have to take it with me. I got a meeting this morning before my conference. See you later.

Yolanda:

Take care.

Belinda:

Was that dad that just left?

Yolanda:

Yes. He said he had a meeting before his conference. He is busy on his grind.

Janice:

Hey you two.

Yolanda:

Hey Mom.

Belinda:

Hey Mom. You off today?

Janice:

Yes. I have a hair appointment this morning.

Yolanda:

What time do you have to be there?

Janice:

I am about to head out in about ten minutes. My appointment is about twenty-five minutes from now.

Yolanda:

I heard you and dad going back and forth. What is really going on?

Janice:

I feel that his attention is elsewhere.

Yolanda:

Mom, you have no solid proof.

Janice:

I just feel that there is something else out there that is catching his interest.

"THE DOORBELL RINGS"

Janice:

Who can that possibly be early this morning?

Yolanda:

It is Lachelle.

Lachelle:

Hey family, how are you all doing?

Yolanda:

We doing pretty good cousin.

Belinda:

I thought I heard you down here. Hey Lachelle.

<u>Lachelle:</u>

Hey cousin.

<u>Janice:</u>

What brings you in the neighborhood?

<u>Lachelle:</u>

I need to talk to you.

<u>Janice:</u>

I don't have time. I have a hair appointment.

<u>Lachelle:</u>

I will ride with you. I had a friend drop me off.

"JANICE AND LACHELLE LEAVES"

<u>Belinda:</u>

Sis, you know what she wants.

<u>Yolanda:</u>

Mom needs to stop this. I do not like when people come around only when they need something. Anyone that mom helps, never does anything in return.

<u>Belinda:</u>

All mom needs to do is quit worrying about what people will think and just say no and keep it moving. Life would be so much easier on her if she just did that. It is a good thing that dad doesn't know any of this. I feel bad because this is not fair to him. Imagine how mom would react if the shoe was on the other foot and he was doing all of this. She would have a fit.

Yolanda:

I know what you mean Sis. I do feel bad for dad and the fact that he doesn't know.

"JANICE & LACHELLE ARRIVES AT THE BEAUTY SALON"

Lachelle:

I really need to borrow some money. I am in a bind.

Janice:

You look like you need your hair done.

Lachelle:

I really do but I be focusing on my kids having before me getting my hair done.

Janice:

Let's go in, we will talk later.

"JANICE & LACHELLE GOES IN"

Janice & Lachelle:

Hello everyone.

Felicia:

Hey there good people.

Myesha & Rhonda:

Hey sis, how are you?

Janice:

Hey. All sisters in one place. How often do you see this?

<u>Tianna:</u>

Is this a girl's day out or what?

<u>Carmen:</u>

I know right. We were long overdue for this.

<u>Felicia:</u>

Ok Janice, what are you getting today?

<u>Janice:</u>

Give me the usual.

<u>Felicia:</u>

Ok, the usual it is.

<u>Myesha:</u>

Now Janice, you should try something different to surprise your husband. You should change it up to spice it up.

<u>Janice:</u>

What do you suggest?

<u>Myesha:</u>

Rhonda, break out that hair magazine.

<u>Lachelle:</u>

I am going to bounce. I got something that I have to get done. Janice, I will catch you later.

<u>Janice:</u>

Ok cousin, take care.

"LACHELLE LEAVES"

Rhonda:

Janice, please tell me that this girl wasn't trying to get money out of you?

Janice:

She needs help.

Myesha:

No! What she need is to stop having all those kids and not getting child support. She tried bumming money from me.

Tianna:

I wasn't going to say anything but she came by my job asking me for money and said not to tell anyone. I gave her twenty dollars so she could get her child that she had with her something to eat.

Rhonda:

What in the world do she have going on? Tianna, please do not give her any more money. I know she is getting money from somewhere but we don't know if she is doing the right thing with it.

Felicia:

She came in about a month ago and got her hair done. When it came time to pay, she had no money. I pulled her outside to talk to here. I told her that this was on me and a gift to you. I told her don't do that again. She was lucky that it was me because with anyone else, she was going to have problems.

Janice:

I cannot believe this girl. She is all over town owing and begging for money. I don't understand knowing that she could have come to me earlier.

Carmen:

She doesn't really approach me because she knows that if she asks me, she would have to come to my place of business and work for it. I wouldn't have her doing anything difficult. She would do something as simple as filing paperwork and running errands like dropping my shipments off to the post office.

Myesha:

Janice, you cannot worry about helping her because you have a family of your own. Don't create a problem for your home.

Rhonda:

Speaking of creating a problem, Dominic told me that you gave him some money. He was mad at me and told me that you were the only one that cared about him. He only said it because I wouldn't give him money when he asked me for it.

Carmen:

Janice, when you started enabling, you already created a problem. That is going to drive a wedge between your marriage. Believe me when I say this, if you continue to enable the behavior, your frustration will be targeted at the wrong person. Your husband is around you more and he would become your first victim of your blowup.

Myesha:

Sis, she is right. Let me ask you this. Are you and De'Andre having any issues?

Janice:

I wouldn't say issues. We have been at each other from time to time. Married couples argue and have disagreements.

Myesha:

Could it be that you went at him in your state of frustration of everyone that you enable?

Felicia:

Janice, you have a good man. Don't mess that up for anything.

Janice:

I don't know. I don't think he really understand where I am coming from. I am only trying to help in every way.

Rhonda:

What good is it to help someone that is not your responsibility and sacrifice losing what should mean the world to you?

Janice:

I know what you mean sis. It is just hard knowing someone need help.

Rhonda:

There is a difference between needing help and helping yourself.

Carmen:

Janice, imagine if the shoe was on the other foot. What if this situation was going on and it was De'Andre enabling his family members? How would you feel if you found out, especially him keeping it from you?

Tianna:

Carmen, you have a great point. I know that I wouldn't be able to take it. It would definitely wreck my nerves. I would be thinking about money that I would consider wasted. Janice, you have to also think about what your response would be to him. Not saying that you will blow up but who knows if the opportunity presented itself.

Myesha:

Sis, you do not need to stress yourself over Lachelle. Don't make her problems your problems.

Janice:

I never look at it like that. I just don't like seeing anyone struggle.

Rhonda:

When all you do is beg and not try on your own, it is not a struggle. It is called looking for a hand out.

Felicia:

Here it is. What do you think Janice?

Janice:

I love it. This hair style definitely fits me.

Tianna:

Truly a new look. I am feeling that right there.

Myesha:

I see you Mrs. magazine model.

Rhonda:

Sis, that is definitely you. The change was overdue.

Janice:

Thank you everyone. I needed this today. Having this moment to myself with my girls is a moment to cherish.

Myesha:

It is important for you to get these moments because this is the time to yourself. You are so wrapped up in helping people that refuses to prioritize their own lives. Sis, that really has to stop. If you continue, you can lose focus on you and what you have going on.

Janice:

I understand sis. I am about to head back home. I have a couple of errands to run. We must do this again.

Felicia:

See you later Janice.

Janice:

You all take care.

Myesha & Rhonda:

See you later Sis.

"JANICE LEAVES"

Tianna:

I know Janice is under a lot of stress because the girl has a heart of gold.

Felicia:

She does have a heart of gold and always had since I have known her.

Carmen:

That's my cousin for you. She is so sweet.

Myesha:

You know what. Me and Rhonda is going to get our sister out for a spa and massage day. Maybe that will help her relax.

Rhonda:

You know that I am down for that.

Carmen:

Let me know, I may go with you all.

"JANICE ARRIVES AT HOME"

Janice:

I am home. Anyone here?

Belinda:

I am here. Yolanda went to meet up with one of her sorority sisters for an upcoming event.

Janice:

Has your day come home yet?

Belinda:

He went over Aunt Syerra's house. He said they were going to discuss getting together to go to nana's grave. I think it is nice that they turn it into a celebration of life. They get together to do things as if they mom was with them. I know that they took her out to her favorite restaurant once a month. Now they gather on the date she passed.

"MEANWHILE OVER AT SYERRA'S HOUSE"

De'Andre:

Hey sis, what do you have to drink"

Syerra:

What do you want?

De'Andre:

Hennessey if you have it.

Syerra:

You in luck. I have a little left. I have to go to the store and stock up.

Miguel:

I am getting one of your Pepsi colas out of the refrigerator.

De'Andre:

I needed this. I haven't had it in a while.

Syerra:

What's on your mind big bruh? You haven't been yourself lately.

Miguel:

I have to agree with you sis. He hasn't been himself.

De'Andre:

Putting a lot of hours at work trying to accomplish my goal. You know how hard it is as a minority trying to establish your importance in the workforce. It comes with hard work and the stress that comes with the job.

Syerra:

I hear you big bruh but there is something else going on with you. How is everything with you and Janice?

De'Andre:

She has been stressing me out about the job and the time that I have been putting in. She was also questioning me about my co-worker Kandace.

Syerra:

Oh really. She thinks that you and her are messing around?

De'Andre:

Sis, to be truthfully honest, I do not know what Janice is thinking. I haven't given her a reason to think anything.

Miguel:

I seen his co-worker Kandace. That girl is fine. I could see why Janice would be a little insecure.

De'Andre:

What ever happened to giving me the benefit of the doubt? You cannot blame me for the way someone looks. Kandace knows my whole family and my daughters are crazy about her. Kandace is not even trying to cross any lines. She is driven like me trying to get a minority business off the ground.

Syerra:

Is she going to be a part of your team once you accomplish getting your own firm?

De'Andre:

Yes she is. Why wouldn't I recruit some of the best in the business? I need people that will help the empire to consistent growth.

Syerra:

You sure that Kandace doesn't have a thing for you?

De'Andre:

I seriously doubt it. She has never approached me in an inappropriate matter.

Syerra:

I ask that question because in some cases, people can have a great working relationship which could be a turn-on to people. Is she married?

De'Andre:

No. She is divorced. Her husband was very abusive and became a heavy drinker. I don't know what the underlying problem was.

Miguel:

A woman with a good job, he truly screwed up. I know if I was looking for a woman, she would be my ideal dream.

Syerra:

You my brother and I know how you feel about your family. Kandace can also look at the fact of you being who you are and taking care of your family. A woman that has been abused can only dream of having what she sees in you. I am just saying, be very observative.

De'Andre:

I hear sis. I don't see her trying to come between me and Janice. Kandace has talked to Janice on numerous occasions. When you see them talking, it is like they are the best of friends.

Miguel:

All I know is if she is looking for a loving and caring man, she doesn't have to look any further.

Syerra:

Miguel, you are my brother. You are a good guy with some funny ways. Remember, you dated a girl at my job. She was suppose to meet up with you. She was five minutes late and you stop calling the girl.

Miguel:

Sis, it wasn't like that. It was more than that. She had issues that no one saw in her. She hid a lot of what happened to her in the past. She was getting help to deal with a lot of what she had going on.

Syerra:

I hear you baby brother.

De'Andre:

What are we deciding to do to celebrate the anniversary of mom going to eternal life? I know we go to her favorite restaurant, but we can also do something else along with that. I was thinking something like personalizing Chinese lanterns with her picture and name on it. WE could read a poem before releasing the lanterns.

Miguel:

I am with that. Truly something different. I figure after we eat, we can do a slideshow after the reading of the poem. I have a lot of pictures that I can gather up.

Syerra:

That will be perfect. Where would a good venue for this event be best?

De'Andre:

We can have it at the house. That way, we can avoid the costly unnecessary expenses.

Syerra:

You think that would be ok knowing there is a little friction with Janice?

De'Andre:

It will be fine. I don't see that posing a problem knowing what the cause is for. This is another way my daughters can pay tribute to their grandmother.

Syerra:

Ok then. It is set.

De'Andre:

Ok everyone. I am on my way home. I will talk to you two later.

"DE'ANDRE LEAVES"

Miguel:

Sis, do you think that it is a good idea to have it at De'Andre's house knowing that some friction is there?

Syerra:

I will say that everything would be fine. I think their friction is something within them that manifest then it disappears. I think that is the ups and downs of a marriage.

Miguel:

I guess that this is why I am not married. I have a very low tolerance for people being very petty. I would be ready to cut my losses up front because that is a use of too much wasted energy.

Syerra:

It is good that you are up front about everything and honest with yourself. Sometimes you may come across people that may meet all those needs. Later on down the line, people may change over time.

"DE'ANDRE ARRIVES HOME"

De'Andre:

I'm home.

Belinda:

Hey dad, how are you?

De'Andre:

I am good. Where is your mom and Yolanda?

<u>Belinda:</u>

Mom is in the shower and Yolanda is over her sorority sister's house. You look tired. Is the workload heavy?

<u>De'Andre:</u>

It is but I can see it diminishing soon. We have been doing end of the quarter reports plus taking on a lot of new accounts that I am trying to assign to what my firm will soon be.

<u>Belinda:</u>

I know you will glad once everything calms down. Your time is coming and before you know it, your business will be taking off the ground.

<u>Janice:</u>

Hey. I thought I heard you downstairs.

<u>De'Andre:</u>

I just got home about fifteen minutes ago.

<u>Belinda:</u>

I am about to turn in. Goodnight mom and dad.

<u>De'Andre & Janice:</u>

Goodnight.

<u>Janice:</u>

What do you and your siblings have planned?

<u>De'Andre:</u>

The celebration for my mother is starting off with us eating and reminiscing at her favorite restaurant. We are also personalizing Chinese lanterns that we are going to release after we read a poem reflecting on her. We are going to have the event right here.

Janice:

Here? Will there be enough room?

De'Andre:

It is not going to be an overabundance of people. Pretty much immediate family and maybe a couple of people from her church.

Janice:

You mind if I have a couple of my family members and maybe some co-workers attend?

De'Andre:

I am fine with that. I want to try and get a head count by the end of the week so I will know how many lanterns to get made.

Janice:

Is Kandace going to be there?

De'Andre:

She doesn't even know about it. What is it about Kandace that bugs you? I don't get you when it comes to her.

Janice:

I was just asking.

De'Andre:

Yeah right. Your attitude changes towards me when it comes to her. You really been trippin hard.

Janice:

No I am not. I was just asking a question. You act like you have something to hide.

De'Andre:

You trying to twist stuff around. I am going to bed. Goodnight.

Janice:

Goodnight then.

END OF SCENE 3

SCENE 4 – ANOTHER DAY AT THE OFFICE:

Janice:

Hey everyone.

Malaysah & Sherise:

Hey girl

Janice:

Where is Jermaine?

Malaysha:

He is out today. He wasn't feeling good.

Janice:

I won't be here the whole day. I need to go and see my cousin Danielle. I have an appointment with her.

Sherise:

Is everything good?

Janice:

She is helping me get through some things.

Malaysha:

Is it something that we can help you with as well?

Janice:

No. I will be good.

Sherise:

You sure Janice, because you do not seem like yourself.

Janice:

Just a couple of things that me and De'Andre are going through. I feel that I don't have his undivided attention. He is working a lot.

<u>Malaysha:</u>

Doesn't that come along with doing what is needed to have your own business?

<u>Janice:</u>

Yes, I guess.

"DOMINIC SHOWS UP TO HER JOB"

<u>Dominic:</u>

Hey sis. Hey everyone.

<u>Janice:</u>

Dominic, what are you doing here?

<u>Dominic:</u>

Sis, I need to speak with you. It is important.

<u>Janice:</u>

Dominic, you need to leave. We will talk later. You cannot be coming by my job like this.

"DOMINIC LEAVES"

"MEANWHILE AT DE'ANDRE'S JOB"

<u>De'Andre:</u>

Hey Kandace, do we have everything we need for the conference? I think this is going to be the one that we will increase the volume of our clients. I can see something that is promising for the future. I can see it now, at least having more than half of these clients in our very own business.

<u>Kandace:</u>

Everything is in place for the presentation. I went over everything twice to make sure that we covered all the key points. I heard that we were also going to have some distinguished guests at this conference.

<u>De'Andre:</u>

That is cool. Anyone you know or heard of in particular?

<u>Kandace:</u>

I heard one was the vice president of the board of directors. Some others are members of the board.

<u>De'Andre:</u>

This should definitely land us the recommendation for us to move forward with our plans of branching off on our own.

<u>Kandace:</u>

We will be landing the ultimate dream.

<u>De'Andre:</u>

Oh, before I forget, we are having a small gathering for celebrating my mother's anniversary of her journey to eternal life. Would you like to join us?

<u>Kandace:</u>

Sure. Count me in.

<u>De'Andre:</u>

I know that my daughters would be glad to see you.

<u>Kandace:</u>

How are they doing? I haven't seen my girls in a little while.

<u>De'Andre:</u>

They are doing great.

<u>Kandace:</u>

How is Janice doing?

<u>De'Andre:</u>

I guess she is doing good.

<u>Kandace:</u>

What's going on? That didn't sound too positive.

<u>De'Andre:</u>

She is on whatever she is on.

<u>Kandace:</u>

That bad?

<u>De'Andre:</u>

I am going to keep it real. She has been tripping about you. Almost every time we get into a conversation, somehow you come up in a conversation indirectly.

<u>Kandace:</u>

What do you mean?

<u>De'Andre:</u>

You know when we are doing something that is work related, she is always inquiring about the long hours when I tell her what we are trying to do. She always tries to twist it into something that it is not.

<u>Kandace:</u>

I am sorry that this is causing you problems. I thought that she would at least be happy about owning your own firm.

De'Andre:

I am pretty sure that she will come around. You have nothing to be sorry about because you didn't do anything.

Kandace:

Okay, I hear you. Are you ready to go into the conference?

De'Andre:

Yes. I am ready to hopefully win influence over this crowd. There will be at least seventy-five people in attendance.

Kandace:

Let's do this.

"DE'ANDRE & KANDACE GOES INTO THE CONFERENCE"

"JANICE MAKES HER WAY TO SEE DANIELLE"

Janice:

Hey Danielle, how are you doing?

Danielle:

I am good. How about you?

Janice:

I have seen better days.

Danielle:

Before we get started, I ran into Lachelle and she was saying that she needed some money. She said that she couldn't get in touch with you. Are you still giving this girl money?

<u>Janice:</u>

It has been a month since the last time she came to me for money.

<u>Danielle:</u>

Janice, that is part of many problems that are there. You have to quit what you are doing. That is going to create major problems.

<u>Janice:</u>

I hear you cousin. I am under a lot of stress. I know most of it, I am causing myself because I want to make sure that everyone is good.

<u>Danielle:</u>

One thing that you have to do is drop the guilt trip. That guilt trip will drive a wedge between your marriage. Are you taking your frustration out on De'Andre?

<u>Janice:</u>

I don't think I am.

<u>Danielle:</u>

Let me rephrase the question. Do you find yourself in disagreement with him most of the time?

<u>Janice:</u>

Yes I do. It is frequently.

<u>Danielle:</u>

Do you know what it is you are in disagreement with?

<u>Janice:</u>

Not all the time.

<u>Danielle:</u>

Can you name at least one? When people are in disagreement, they should know what it is about unless you are the one always disagreeing majority of the time.

Janice:

I disagree with the fact that he is putting in all these hours at work.

Danielle:

Didn't you say that he is trying to start his own firm?

Janice:

Yes he is. It just bothers me that he is putting in all these hours.

Danielle:

What is the real problem? Would it happen to be his co-worker?

Janice:

He spends a lot of time with her.

Danielle:

If that is going to be his business partner, wouldn't it take them being on the same page about the business at all times? Do you fully support his endeavors?

Janice:

I guess so. I do support him.

Danielle:

Do you think he feels that you do? Keep in mind, he may not think that because there are more disagreements than agreements.

Janice:

I'll try my best.

Danielle:

First thing that you need to do is to quit jumping on him about his co-worker when you are feeling insecure. Your insecurity is not justification. Next, support him more than you do other family members. Quit being their enablers. They are taking your focus away from what is most important. Janice, you are my cousin and I know you. Deep down, you are contributing to the fact of you being unhappy.

Janice:

I get what you are saying. I know that I have to do better at working on me.

Danielle:

Trust me when I say things. Things will get better only if you allow it to. Eliminate a lot of distractions and you will be fine.

Janice:

I promise you that I will work on it. I know that I have to work harder when it comes to my husband. He is taking care of everything. I will say that I do have it made.

Danielle:

Having it made like that, you definitely need to be taking care of him. With all the hard work that he is putting in to increase the income in the home, supporting him will be a no brainer.

Janice:

Cousin, you have my word. I take everything that you are saying into consideration. I have to go back to the office. I forgot about some reports I meant to bring home. Thank you again for squeezing me in.

Danielle:

No problem cousin. I will talk with you later.

"JANICE LEAVES"

"DE'ANDRE AND KANDACE COMES OUT OF THE CONFERENCE"

De'Andre:

Kandace, I think we secured the deal with future business with some heavy hitters. I think that the presentation captured all the points we were trying to convey to our target audience. Thank you so much for putting together a well-organized presentation.

Kandace:

It was my pleasure. It was a team effort because you provided all the information.

De'Andre:

I understand but you were the one that put everything in sequence. You already had the key points they were looking for.

Kandace:

At least we got the major part of the presentation out of the way. Now all we have to do is present them with all the procedures and protocols that we have set in place.

De'Andre:

Man, that is what I am talking about. I can see the business taking off now. About to go home and share the news with the family.

Kandace:

I heard that. I am going to pick up my niece. I told my sister that I would watch her while her and her husband go out and celebrate his birthday. I will see you tomorrow.

De'Andre:

Ok. Be safe and take care.

"DE'ANDRE AND KANDACE LEAVES THE CONFERENCE"

"JANICE ARRIVES AT HER JOB"

Sherise:

Hey Janice, I thought you were gone for the rest of the day.

Janice:

There were some documents I meant to take home so I came back to get them. Why are you still here?

Sherise:

I wanted to finish up my end of the quarter reports. I have already gotten everything started for the next quarter. How did you visit go with your cousin?

Janice:

It went pretty well. I have a long way to go because I have a lot on my mind. I understood what she was saying to me, but she doesn't understand how I feel.

Sherise:

What is it that she doesn't understand? Did you tell her everything you needed to tell her?

Janice:

I feel I did.

"LACHELLE SHOWS UP TO HER JOB"

Lachelle:

Hey cousin, I really need to talk to you.

Janice:

How did you get here?

Lachelle:

A friend of mine brought me here. They are outside.

Janice:

What is it that you need Lachelle?

Lachelle:

I need to hold some money until my money from child support come in.

Janice:

What is it that you are doing with your money? Here it is, you are needing money for the kids but I am looking at your hair and your nails.

Lachelle:

My neighbor does this for me. We do favors for each other. I will watch her two kids when she needs to run errands. She also uses me as one of her models to display in her portfolio to show clients. To me, it is an even trade because I cannot afford this at all. I just need a little something until I get my payment.

Janice:

Alright Lachelle. I cannot continue to do this. You need to improve on whatever it is you are doing.

Lachelle:

I hear you cousin. I appreciate it. I promise that I am going to work harder at this.

"LACHELLE LEAVES"

Sherise:

Can I ask you something Janice?

Janice:

Sure you can.

Sherise:

What you just did, was that part of the conversation you had with Danielle?

Janice:

Some of the conversation.

Sherise:

Janice, I have known you for a little while. You have been giving this girl money as far back as I can remember. You know that has been a problem from the start.

Janice:

I am trying to keep the problem to a minimum.

Sherise:

Janice this should have stopped a long time ago. How would you honestly feel if De'Andre was doing this? Also, think about it like this. What if he was doing this and kept it a secret? You would not like that one bit.

Janice:

You are right. I know that there are some people that I have to cut off and quit catering to. I have always been that one that don't like to see anyone suffer.

Sherise:

People don't have to suffer when all they have to do is make better choices. Also, it is not your obligation nor your responsibility for what everyone else is doing or the decision they make. Girl, let's get out of here. We got to be here tomorrow morning.

Janice:

Alright girl, I will see you tomorrow.

Sherise:

Take care.

"JANICE LEAVES"

"DE'ANDRE ARRIVES AT HOME"

De'Andre:

Hey you two, how are you two doing?

Yolanda:

I'm doing good.

Belinda:

Everything is great.

Yolanda:

How are things coming along with the business venture?

De'Andre:

Everything is coming along just great. This last presentation that we just presented to this last group. I am pretty confident that we will have their business. I would say in about a few months, we should be up and going.

Belinda:

That is great. Do I have a position reserved for me in the firm?

De'Andre:

As a matter of fact, there is a guaranteed position for the both of you. It would be nice to have both of my daughters at my firm.

Yolanda:

That would be nice to have something to call our own and carry out our legacy.

De'Andre:

This is only the beginning.

Belinda:

How is the planning coming for Grandma's celebration anniversary?

De'Andre:

Everything is in order and ready to go.

Yolanda:

I am looking forward to it.

"JANICE ARRIVES HOME WITH HER GRANDMOTHER"

Janice:

Hey everyone. Look who I have been hanging out with.

Yolanda:

Hey grandma. How have you been?

Belinda:

Hey grandma.

Mildred:

Hey my babies. Yall come give this old lady a hug.

De'Andre:

Hey Mrs. Mildred. Long time no see.

Mildred:

Hey baby. How is work treating you?

De'Andre:

Mrs. Mildred, everything is going great. All my plans are coming into existence. Pretty soon in the near future, I will have my own firm.

Mildred:

That is outstanding. Dreams do come true. God is on your side. It is destined and it will happen.

De'Andre:

The man upstairs has truly been a blessing.

Yolanda:

Grandma, you staying the night with us? We are having fajitas tonight.

Mildred:

I am definitely staying and you can count me in for fajitas.

De'Andre:

Dinner will be done in a few. Let me get your bag so I can take it up to the room.

Mildred:

Thank you baby. You are so sweet.

Yolanda:

Grandma, I am going to make sure that you get a ticket to my graduation. I will be graduating with a BS as a Registered Nurse.

Mildred:

Count me in. I am there. How long do you have Belinda?

Belinda:

I have a couple of years left. I changed my major to Finance. I was previously going for architect.

Mildred:

I am so proud of the both of you. Janice, I know that you are a proud mother.

Janice:

Yes I am.

Yolanda:

The food is ready.

Mildred:

Just to think, your husband is about to own his own firm.

Janice:

He been working at it.

Mildred:

These fajitas are good. Someone put they foot in these.

Belinda:

Dad made these. He loves to cook.

Mildred:

I see. I am going to have to come over more often for dinner.

De'Andre:

You are more than welcome to come over Mrs. Mildred. I also have lemon pound cake for dessert.

<u>Mildred:</u>

You are going to have me coming over all the time. I might as well move in.

<u>Yolanda:</u>

Grandma, I know what you mean. Dad be throwing down in the kitchen.

<u>Belinda:</u>

I am stuffed. I am about to knock out these dishes.

<u>Yolanda:</u>

I will help you. I am going to clear the table.

<u>De'Andre:</u>

I am going up to get my stuff ready for tomorrow and take a shower.

<u>Janice:</u>

Ok. Me and Grandma is going into the living room to watch tv.

<u>Yolanda:</u>

Me and Belinda are going to catch a movie with some friends. We will be back later.

<u>Janice:</u>

Have fun.

<u>Mildred:</u>

Enjoy yourselves.

"YOLANDA AND BELINDA LEAVES"

<u>Mildred:</u>

Babygirl, we need to talk.

Janice:

What's on your mind Grandma?

Mildred:

I have been watching you and you have not said anything, especially about your husband's accomplishments. You should be on cloud nine just like he is. What's going on?

Janice:

Nothing is going on Grandma.

Mildred:

I may be an old lady but I am not an old fool. You are not showing a whole lot of support from what I see. I watched your body language and you two were not in sequence.

Janice:

I am not really familiar of what he does other than knowing what his job is. He talks about it and I listen.

Mildred:

That is not what I am talking about. You just do not seem to interested in what he is trying to do.

Janice:

We have talked. I told him that I wasn't crazy about the hours that he was putting in.

Mildred:

Baby, that is just part of owning a future business. Having problems with his hours is showing no support. Another thing, you need to stop giving money to Dominic and Lachelle. Neither one of them cannot keep their mouths closed. Too many people know your business. I am just surprised that De'Andre doesn't know.

Janice:

I wanted to make sure that they had what they needed for the kids.

Mildred:

You wrong for that and that is not your responsibility. You are doing things that is going to make your husband resent you. Baby, you have a good man. Don't mess that up for anything. I want you to sit back and think hard about it.

Janice:

I hear you Grandma. I will think about everything you said. You never guided me wrong. It is getting late. Got to get ready for tomorrow. It's the big day tomorrow. The releasing of the tribute lanterns for De'Andre's mother.

Mildred:

I am looking forward to the celebration. I know that he went all out. See you in the morning.

END OF SCENE 4

SCENE 5 – MOVING TOWARDS FUTURE CHALLENGES:

"EVERYONE IS IN ATTENDANCE FOR THE GATHERING"

De'Andre:

I want to take this moment and thank everyone that is here in attendance for the celebration anniversary of my mother's life. For anyone that personally knew her, you can say that she was truly an angel in every way. She would give the shirt off of her back for anyone that needed clothing. She was truly special to everyone. Because of her, I am where I am today. She always pushed me to be the best at what I do. I am not going to hold the floor. I am going to pass it to my brother Miguel.

Miguel:

Again, like my brother said. I want to thank everyone for attending our special event. I know my mother would have loved to see everyone come out for her. She was truly my rock. She definitely instilled integrity in us all. Without her, I would not be where I am at now. Passing it to my sister Syerra.

Syerra:

Good morning everyone. Thank you all for coming out. Seeing you all warms my heart. It shows that you all lover here and I am truly grateful for that. She taught me a lot especially how to love ad open your heart to people. Don't get me wrong, no one was going to run over her. She was what I called the definition of caring. There are a few others that would like to speak.

Yolanda:

My grandmother was definitely an inspiration to me. She was the one that influenced me to join the Divine Nine. She represented the Pretty Poodles of Sigma Gamma Rho. She wore her Royal Blue and Gold proudly. I was her biggest fan. Hey sis, come over and share your memory.

<u>Belinda:</u>

To kind of piggy back off of what my sister was saying, she was my inspiration to joining the Divine Nine. She always told me that the skies the limit. She always said, baby no matter what, aim for the stars.

<u>De'Andre:</u>

Again, I want to thank everyone for coming. This celebration symbolizes to us that my mother is always here no matter what. The sending off of the lanterns is our way of communicating with our loved ones letting them know that our love is everlasting and unconditional. You are never forgotten. I would like to bring up Mrs. Mildred. She is my wife's grandmother and the matriarch of the family. Mrs. Mildred, we would be honored if you would light the lanterns.

<u>Mildred:</u>

I don't know what to say. I am truly honored that you all chose me.

<u>Syerra:</u>

Me and my brothers talked about it and came to the conclusion of letting a woman with so much wisdom send off this dedication to another woman with so much wisdom.

"MILDRED LIGHTS THE LANTERNS"

<u>De'Andre:</u>

Before we release the lanterns, I have a poem I will like to read. I call this poem "Our Mother" "Our Bridgebuilder"

The lighting of the memory lantern

It signifies the heartbeat of our love,

We know that you watch over us

From the Heavens way up above.

An Abundance of unconditional love

You taught us all each day,

We return the same type of love

Each and every time we pray.

Your memories will be with us forever

We will remember your special touch,

The love you share all over our lives

Not realizing to this day, that it meant so much.

This concludes our dedication as we release the memory lanterns.

"THE MEMORY LANTERNS ARE BEING RELEASED"

<u>Syerra:</u>

That is so beautiful. I know mom would have cried with us coming together for such a celebration.

<u>Miguel:</u>

I know right. This really touched my heart.

<u>De'Andre:</u>

Hey Mrs. Mildred, I want to introduce you to my co-worker and future business partner Kandace.

<u>Kandace:</u>

It is very nice to meet you Mrs. Mildred. I have heard so much about you.

<u>Mildred:</u>

Hey there Suga, it is very nice to meet you.

<u>Kandace:</u>

De'Andre, sorry that I have to leave so soon. Swinging by my sister's house. They invited me over for dinner. I am going to say hello to the girls before I leave out. See you on Monday.

<u>De'Andre:</u>

Ok Kandace. Thank you again for coming.

<u>Yolanda:</u>

Hey Kandace, girl give me a hug. How are you doing?

<u>Kandace:</u>

Just great. I was just getting ready to come find you and your sister before I left. I have a prior engagement.

<u>Belinda:</u>

Hey Kandace, you about to head out?

<u>Kandace:</u>

Hey Belinda. Yes I am. I have a prior engagement I promised to catch up and do lunch with you two. Take care and I will talk to you later.

<u>Yolanda & Belinda:</u>

See you later.

<u>Mildred:</u>

She seems like a sweet girl.

<u>Yolanda:</u>

She is really down to earth.

<u>Janice:</u>

Hey Grandma, I want to introduce you to my co-workers Malaysha, Sherise and Jermaine.

Mildred:

Nice to meet you all.

Malaysha, Sherise & Jermaine:

The pleasure is all ours.

Malaysha:

Oh my God, that is a beautiful necklace.

Mildred:

Thank you. De'Andre and Janice got if for me on my birthday.

Sherise:

That was truly thoughtful of the both of them. They have great taste.

Mildred:

Thank you

Janice:

You all want to get something to eat? I got the food in the family room.

Jermaine:

You are definitely speaking my language.

Miguel:

We have drinks in the coolers on ice.

Janice:

Syerra, when is your next class? I may have to show up for your next class.

Syerra:

I got a class next week. I can go ahead and slate you in since I still have some openings.

<u>Janice:</u>

Ok cool, I am looking forward to it.

<u>Sherise:</u>

Please slate me in as well.

<u>Syerra:</u>

I got you.

<u>Malaysha:</u>

You might as well include me so we can have a girl's day out.

<u>Janice:</u>

I will check with my cousins Carmen and Danielle to see if they are up for it.

<u>Syerra:</u>

Ok cool. The more, the marrier.

<u>Mildred:</u>

Can an old lady like myself come as well?

<u>Syerra:</u>

Mrs. Mildred, I have a VIP pass for you. That consists of after three visits, you receive a free smoothie and a small snack of your choice.

<u>Mildred:</u>

I definitely have to show up now.

<u>Syerra:</u>

You are always welcome Mrs. Mildred.

<u>Miguel:</u>

Well good people, I am going to get out of here. I got some errands to run. I will catch you all later.

<u>Everyone:</u>

Take care. See you later.

<u>Syerra:</u>

De'Andre and Janice, I know yall have some music. Turn on one of your playlists.

<u>Janice:</u>

Let me find the remote so I can turn on some grown folk music.

"MUSIC COMES ON & EVERYONE GETS UP TO DANCE"

<u>Mildred:</u>

Now that is what I am talking about.

<u>Yolanda:</u>

That is my jam right there.

<u>Mildred:</u>

Baby, what you know about that old school?

<u>Yolanda:</u>

Grandma, me and Belinda be listening to all the old school playlist that they have in their library.

<u>Belinda:</u>

Grandma, I even downloaded some of their stuff so I will have something to listen to when I am out and about or working out.

<u>Malaysha:</u>

I am going to have to get a copy of that playlist. Janice, you should have brought your playlist to the office.

<u>Sherise:</u>

Now you know, with this playlist we would not get anything done.

<u>Jermaine:</u>

Yes we would. It would definitely make time go by faster.

<u>Janice:</u>

I will download a few playlists so we can have at work.

<u>Sherise:</u>

That will be nice. We are about to head out before it starts raining. I heard that it is suppose to rain the rest of the night and you know people do not know how to drive in the rain.

<u>Malaysha:</u>

Girl, you are right. Everything was truly nice. That was a beautiful send off for his mo. I also thought that it was really nice that they had Mrs. Mildred light the lantern.

<u>Janice:</u>

That was a very nice gesture. I had no idea that they were going to do that. My husband is full of surprises.

<u>Malaysha:</u>

Keep what you just said in mind. When you don't know what your husband is up to, his actions prove good intentions. Think about it. We about to leave. You take care.

<u>Janice:</u>

By you all. See you later.

De'Andre:

I am about to take Syerra home. She rode with Miguel.

Syerra:

I need to go by the grocery store to pick up a couple of things.

Yolanda:

Can you drop me and Belinda over a friend's house? We are going to stay over.

De'Andre:

Now I am becoming an uber driver (chuckles). Alright you all, I am ready.

Syerra:

See you later Mrs. Mildred and Janice.

Yolanda & Belinda:

See you later Mom and Grandma

Mildred:

Take care babies.

Janice:

See you two later.

"DE'ANDRE, SYERRA & HIS DAUGHTERS LEAVE"

Mildred:

Now that everyone is gone, I can really talk to you. What is going on with you? Before you answer, let me put it to you like this. I watched you the whole time looking at Kandace like you can burn a hole through her.

Janice:

You see how she looks? She is going to be business partners with De'Andre.

Mildred:

So, you are worried about how this woman look? Just because she works with your husband. You punishing him for that? I have seen how you have been short-tempered with him.

Janice:

I am just a little insecure when it comes to Kandace. I see the attention she gets and I am wondering if she has gotten De'Andre's attention.

Mildred:

So, the fact that you are a little insecure, you are blaming De'Andre for this? I see the way you have towards him. I can tell by the way that you were looking at Kandace that you did not want her here.

Janice:

She hasn't personally done anything to me that I know of. I say it like that because I am not around her.

Mildred:

Now Janice, you know that she hasn't did anything to you. Talking about not that you know of, do you honestly think that she would spend time doing something underhanded towards you? One thing that I noticed is she is very fond of your daughters and they seem to be crazy about her. I am pretty sure that if something was going on, Yolanda and Belinda would have picked up on something.

Janice:

Yeah. I guess you are right.

Mildred:

Quit paying attention to how beautiful she is. From what I see, De'Andre has not treated you any different.

"THE DOORBELL RINGS"

Janice:

I wonder who that is. I am not expecting anyone. It is Dominic.

Dominic:

Hey sis, how are you?

Mildred:

Hey Dominic, is she the only one you are seeing?

Dominic:

No Ma'am. Hey Grandma. I didn't know that you were here.

Mildred:

What brings you by?

Dominic:

Just stopping by to see my sister.

Mildred:

If you say so Dominic.

Dominic:

I was just in the neighborhood stopping by to see one of my kids.

Mildred:

How many kids do you have?

Dominic:

I have three.

"DOORBELL RINGS"

Janice:

It is Rhonda.

Rhonda:

Hey everyone.

Dominic:

My ride is outside. I am about to leave. By everyone.

Rhonda:

How is everything Grandma?

Mildred:

Everything is great. Where are you on your way to?

Rhonda:

Just getting off of work and figured that I would stop over and grab me a plate. Sorry that I couldn't be here for the celebration.

Janice:

Sis, don't worry about it. We understand that you had to work.

Rhonda:

When I get home, I am jumping in a bubble bath. Sis, what was Dominic here for?

Mildred:

I think he had other intentions until he realized that I was here. I know that he was here for some money.

Rhonda:

I kind of figured that. Janice, do not give him anything. I came across one of his kid's mother and she told me that he hasn't been to see his daughter in over a year. She had to have a same day procedure done and the mother wanted to let him know. His daughter is doing great.

Janice:

That is good that she is doing great. Dominic should be ashamed of himself.

Rhonda:

What do you two have planned tomorrow?

Janice:

After church, we are going to throw something on the grill.

Rhonda:

Oh my God. Count me in. What do I need to bring?

Janice:

Just show up. We have plenty of food.

Rhonda:

Sure will. See yall tomorrow.

Mildred:

Take care baby.

Janice:

See you tomorrow.

Mildred:

I am about to go to bed. We will continue our conversation some time tomorrow.

Janice:

Ok. Goodnight.

"NEXT AFTERNOON AFTER CHURCH"

Mildred:

That pastor preached that word today.

Janice:

Yes he did. He threw down.

Rhonda:

That choir did it for me as well.

Mildred:

Yes indeed. They also sung one of my favorite songs.

De'Andre:

I wish I had everything that they sung today as a playlist with them singing.

Janice:

I think the pastor records everything so I can check with him and see if he has it.

De'Andre:

Ok thanks. That will be great. I am about to grab this stuff and get the grill to going. I will be in the back if anyone needs me.

Janice:

Ok.

Rhonda:

Make sure that one of those ribeye steaks have my name on it (chuckles).

Mildred:

What else are we having Janice?

Janice:

We are having baked beans, potato salad, roasted corn on the cob, collard greens and Syerra is bringing some peach cobbler.

Mildred:

I am ready to eat right now because everything sounds so good.

"DOORBELL RINGS"'

Janice:

It is Myesha yall.

Myesha:

Hey everyone. Long time no see.

Janice:

Hey sis, you were able to get a break from the hospital.

Myesha:

Yes. We have been short-staffed like crazy. Don't get me wrong, I enjoy the hours and making the money. I do need some down time.

Mildred:

Hey baby, it's been a long time. How are you doing?

Myesha:

Hey Grandma, everything is wonderful. You are looking good.

Mildred:

Thank you baby. I try to exercise every opportunity that I get.

Myesha:

It is definitely working for you.

Rhonda:

Girl, you better come give me a hug. I have not seen you in a minute. I know that hospital has you busy.

Myesha:

A lot of times, they have me just about everywhere. The fact that I got a day off was a blessing. The thing that is even better is getting food off the grill and being about to hang out with the family.

Mildred:

It is good that you got some time off, especially with everything that is going on. I know the medical world's biggest fights and challenges are all the covid cases. I know that you are but please be careful.

Myesha:

I will Grandma, I promise. I am not trying to get sick by any means.

Rhonda:

I know what you mean. That is why I go straight home after work. You know that there are people out here that still don't wash their hands.

Myesha:

It is even worse seeing it in the medical field among my co-workers which would be one of the first line of defense to help getting people better. I had to call this girl out last week. She doesn't even talk to me anymore. I don't care. IF you are not practicing what we all were taught, then stay away from me.

Mildred:

I am glad that you called her out. Being silent about it doesn't make it any better. People just do not realize how much more danger you can put someone in because of their immune system.

De'Andre:

The food is ready. It is about that time to throw down. Mrs. Mildred, you are first to get your plate.

"DOORBELL RINGS"

Janice:

It's Syerra. Hey girl, you are right on time. The food is ready plus you have what everyone is looking for. The peach cobbler is the finishing touch.

Syerra:

I am here with the peach cobbler everyone.

Rhonda:

Now that is what I am talking about. I will be cheating on my diet today.

Syerra:

Where is Miguel?

Janice:

He is stopping to pick up your nieces on the way here. He should be here within the next ten to fifteen minutes.

Rhonda:

This steak is on point. De'Andre, you put your foot in this. It is perfectly seasoned. Syerra, this peach cobbler is about to put me to sleep. Janice, I am so glad you had some vanilla ice cream.

Myesha:

Girl, you are not lying. This is that food that make you want to go to sleep. I am claiming the couch if I can't drive (chuckles).

Rhonda:

Not if I beat you to it (chuckles).

Mildred:

I am about to get a second helping of potato salad.

De'Andre:

Help yourself Mrs. Mildred. We have plenty of it.

"DOOR OPENS"

Yolanda:

Everyone in here getting their grub on. Hey everyone.

Belinda:

Hey family. All the food smells good.

Miguel:

Hey everyone.

Mildred:

Hey baby. Glad you are here. Plenty of food in the other room.

Rhonda:

Make sure if you don't do anything, get you some of that peach cobbler.

Myesha:

If it is not gone before they get to it.

"DOORBELL RINGS"

Janice:

It's my co-workers

Jermaine:

Hey everyone, we can smell the food all the way down the street.

Sherise:

I know that I am at the right place. How is everyone doing?

Everyone:

We are all good. This food has us all lazy.

Malaysha:

Hey everyone. My favorite time of the day. Anytime that there are good food and good people is my favorite time.

Mildred:

Everything is good, trust me.

Jermaine:

Someone just pulled up in front of the house in a black Audi.

Yolanda:

That is Kandace. I'll open the door.

Sherise:

Hey Janice, you good?

Janice:

I am good.

Sherise:

I am only asking because I was the only one that caught the look on your face when Kandace name was said.

Janice:

No, seriously I am good.

Sherise:

Ok, if you say so.

"KANDACE WALKS IN"

Kandace:

Hello everyone.

Everyone:

Hello Kandace.

Kandace:

Oh my God, the food smells great.

Mildred:

Baby, you better get you a plate before it is all gone.

Kandace:

I definitely will Mrs. Mildred.

Malaysha:

What is that perfume you are wearing?

Kandace:

I can't remember, but it is something new that came out that my sister gave me. I will have to ask her and let you know.

Malaysha:

Yes please. I love it.

Kandace:

Not a problem.

Miguel:

Hey gorgeous, we meet again.

Kandace:

Boy, you so silly. How have you been?

Miguel:

I have been great. You all are doing your thang at the firm.

Kandace:

I have always been a firm believer of extreme hard work truly pays off.

Miguel:

I couldn't agree with you more.

Mildred:

I know what you mean. Forty years of productive service in the medical profession.

Myesha:

Grandma, because of you I am a nurse today. You inspired me.

Mildred:

Thank you baby. Hopefully I can inspire many more.

De'Andre:

Everybody get enough to eat?

Everyone:

Yes indeed.

De'Andre:

I am glad everyone enjoyed everything. I want everyone to get a glass of champaign so we can celebrate this announcement that I have.

Miguel:

I will grab the champaign.

<u>Belinda:</u>

Her are the glasses.

<u>Syerra:</u>

Hey Miguel, I will help you pour them in the glasses.

<u>Miguel:</u>

Alright De'Andre, everyone has their glass.

<u>De'Andre:</u>

Thank you Miguel. I wanted to announce that I now own my own firm. It has been a long time coming. I want to also thank my co-worker Kandace who is now my business partner. We both individually have close to twenty years of experience in the field. I know that my mom is smiling down on me rejoicing.

<u>Mildred:</u>

Congratulations on this milestone. Well-deserved accomplishment to you.

<u>Everyone:</u>

That is great. This is definitely worth celebrating.

<u>Kandace:</u>

This is truly my dream come true. I have to share this information with my mother. I am about to swing by her house before I head home. Thank you for the invite and the great news. See you all later.

<u>Everyone:</u>

Take care Kandace.

<u>Miguel:</u>

Big brother, I know you are about to make major moves.

De'Andre:

Looking forward to making a mark in the world.

Janice:

I am glad that you got what it is you have been wanting.

De'Andre:

This celebration is not just about me. This is a celebration for us. I am hoping that it is something we want together.

Janice:

That wasn't what I meant saying it the way I said it.

De'Andre:

Don't worry about it.

Syerra:

Big brother, I am about to leave. I have a class in the morning that I have to get prepared for. Half of the group I am teaching are brand new to the area and the fitness world. I will talk with you later.

De'Andre:

Take care Sis.

Malaysha, Sherise & Jermaine:

We about to head out ourselves. Janice, we will see you at work tomorrow. You all take care.

Everyone:

Take care everyone.

Rhonda & Myesha:

We are leaving as well. We got us a to-go plate (chuckles)

Janice:

You two take care.

Mildred:

Baby, where is your sister?

Belinda:

She is helping Dad putting up food and taking out trash. I am about to go and help so I can get in the shower and go to bed.

Mildred:

Oh ok. I am about to go back in the living room and talk with your mom.

Belinda:

Is she ok? She wasn't herself. Me and Yolanda noticed it.

Mildred:

She is ok. Her mind gets to wondering about the wrong thing at times.

Belinda:

Let me guess. Is it Kandace?

Mildred:

Part of it but it is something else as well.

Belinda:

Oh ok. Don't be too hard on her.

Mildred:

I promise I won't. Janice, are you in the living room?

Janice:

Yes I am Grandma.

Mildred:

Are we going to talk about tonight?

Janice:

What are you talking about Grandma?

Mildred:

You weren't yourself tonight, basically like the other night we were talking. You seemed find after we got home from church. I've seen a shift after people were arriving in the later part of the day. I specifically seen a mood change after Kandace arrived. Why are you worried about that girl?

Janice:

It is not so much just her. Dominic did not show up.

Mildred:

Why are you surprised about that? All he would do is hound you for money anyway. Janice, do he owe you money? Is that why you are upset?

Janice:

Grandma, he does owe me money. He owes me a lot. Some of my bills are going to fall behind.

Mildred:

Janice, I told you about him and Lachelle. Why are you still enabling them? Now you have put yourself in a bind. Do De'Andre know?

Janice:

No he doesn't. He would be extremely furious.

Mildred:

He would have every right to. Let me ask you this. How much does Lachelle owe you?

Janice:

How do you figure that Lachelle owe me money?

Mildred:

If she didn't owe you anything, you would have simply said that she owes you nothing.

"DOORBELL RINGS"

Janice:

Who could it be this late? It is my friend Tianna.

Tianna:

Hey Janice and Mrs. Mildred. I didn't mean to drop in so late, but I wanted to tell you that Lachelle is in some type of trouble. I've seen her and her dude at it nonstop. It looked like they have been fighting.

Mildred:

Where did you see her at?

Tianna:

Downtown down the street from my office. She was trying to get some money from me. Looking at her, she looked like she had been struggling.

Mildred:

Baby, she can be in a lot of mess. No telling what she is into. I will definitely pray for her.

Tianna:

I am about to get out of here. Got an early morning appointment coming in.

Janice:

Ok, thanks for coming by. Before you leave, get you a plate.

Tianna:

Girl, thank you for that. Now I have something for lunch tomorrow. I will talk with you later. Take care Mrs. Mildred.

Mildred:

Take care baby. Janice, that was nice of her to let you know. What was going on. It goes back to the question of Lachelle owing you some money?

Janice:

Grandma, I cannot lie. Yes she does.

Mildred:

That is going to cause a problem. Let me say this before turning in. Your husband is a good man and he make sure that his family is taken care of. You must do everything that you can to avoid causing any friction in your marriage.

Janice:

You are right Grandma. I have a mess that I need to fix.

Mildred:

Just remember, if you are trying to fix someone else's mess and it will create a mess for you, stay far away from it.

Janice:

I agree with you Grandma.

Mildred:

Ok, let's get some sleep.

Janice:

Ok Grandma. Goodnight.

Mildred:

Goodnight.

"NEXT MORNING AT DE'ANDRE'S FIRM"

De'Andre:

The day has finally come that we can say that we got our own firm.

Kandace:

I still cannot believe it. Now we are the competition to our former employer. I know that this is not going to be an easy journey but with time, I know everything will come together.

De'Andre:

I am looking forward to that. Do we have all the documents for the meetings? I know that we will be acquiring a few more accounts today. We have about an hour before going in.

Kandace:

We have everything. Before we go in, is everything ok with you? You do not seem like yourself.

De'Andre:

I am good. Why do you say that?

Kandace:

We have been doing this for a long time. Every conference that we have had, your eagerness was always through the roof and you always have your game face on. Right now, I am not seeing it in an individual whose dream was to own a firm. I know something is going on.

De'Andre:

It is just some personal issues. The communication between me and Janice has been very sketchy and limited. It is like at times once a conversation starts, it begins to head south before we really get into the depth of the conversation.

Kandace:

Do you think there is a little stress from both sides? What I am saying is thinking about the time you put into getting to this point is stressful enough. Then from her perspective, all the hours gone and not home a lot may be putting stress on her.

De'Andre:

That is a possibility but regardless, I do not limit myself to communicating with her. Sometimes she gets in her moods that becomes unbearable at times. The only thing I can do is get away for a little bit.

Kandace:

Have you tried talking to her expressing how you feel?

De'Andre:

We have talked before on a couple of occasions. Most of the time, we do not really come to a conclusion. Sometimes, I just think that she chooses to have her understanding as if she is purposely doing this.

Kandace:

We can definitely chat more about this and maybe I can give some helping hints, but now let's get ready for our first official meeting.

De'Andre:

You are right. Let's do this.

"MEANWHILE AT JANICE'S JOB"

Malaysha:

Janice, you all threw down yesterday.

Sherise:

If you still have any food left, you can definitely send it my way. You know that I try to avoid cooking if possible.

Jermaine:

I am finishing my leftovers for lunch today. I need for De'Andre to share his secret for the marinade on the steaks.

Janice:

I am glad that you enjoyed the food. It is almost all gone.

Sherise:

Alright Janice, give us the rundown. What is going on with you and don't say nothing?

Janice:

I have no idea what you are talking about.

Malaysha:

Janice, we noticed that you really do not do much communicating with your husband. We do not see you two really connecting like you two did when you first met.

Janice:

There has been a lot going on. He had been putting in so many hours at work.

Sherise:

Well think about it Janice, that comes with the territory of starting your own business. Did you not expect that?

Janice:

I don't know.

Malaysha:

It is something deeper than that. Is it his business partner?

Janice:

It is not her. I did think about the hours he spent with her.

Malaysha:

Ok, now I see. Part of the problem is that you are insecure. From what I see, De'Andre does not give me the vibe as giving you something to worry about.

Sherise:

Are you sure that you are telling us everything? Something is not really adding up. For someone that has been in the business with your husband for that long, why haven't he left you years ago? We are talking about a woman who has everything going for herself.

Janice:

Sherise, I agree. I have nothing solid to go on.

Jermaine:

Janice, you have a visitor. I am going to the front and escort them in.

Janice:

Ok cool. Thank you Jermaine.

Malaysha:

Janice, if you can say that you have nothing solid, what makes you so insecure?

Janice:

They just seem to be close. I know that they have worked together for years. At times, I think it is more than just that.

Malaysha:

I wouldn't jump the gun if I was you.

Dominic:

Hey Sis.

Janice:

Dominic, what are you doing here?

Dominic:

I need to talk to you.

Janice:

You cannot be coming up to my job. You got the nerve to show your face when you were suppose to be at my house yesterday.

Dominic:

Sis, quit trippin and listen.

Janice:

Wait a minute. Who are you talking to like that? You better go back and find out where you lost your mind at.

Dominic:

I am talking to you.

Jermaine:

Hey Dominic. It is time for you to go. Either you can go on your own or I can have security escort you out of here.

Malaysha:

Dominic, you need to apologize to your sister for grabbing her arm.

Janice:

Dominic, just go. Jermaine, please walk him out.

Jermaine:

Come on Dominic, let's go.

Sherise:

That is a shame. Janice, has he ever blown up at you like that?

Janice:

Not really.

Sherise:

Janice, do not make any excuses for him. It is a reason that he did it and whatever it is, the excuse is unacceptable. The way he grabbed your arm tells me that this is not the first time. It also tells me the reason why he is not with any of the mothers of his children.

Malaysha:

Girl, look at your arm. How are you going to hide those marks? You know that your husband and your grandmother is going to see it.

Janice:

I will figure out some way. I will wear a shirt with sleeves.

Malaysha:

You need to quit covering up for someone that will possibly hurt you seriously because they can't get what they want out of you. Janice, you really need to tell your husband what happened.

Sherise:

Janice, I agree with Malaysah. You don't want your husband to find out in a way that it will catch him off guard.

Janice:

I have to figure out a way without my husband going off on the deep end. Let's go grab some lunch so I can clear my mind.

Malaysha:

I am with that. We can grab Jermaine on the way out.

"JANICE & HER CO-WORKERS HEAD OUT FOR LUNCH"

"MEANWHILE, DE'ANDRE FINISHES UP THE FIRST PART OF HIS MEETING"

Kandace:

Well, we knocked that out of the park. The people that are staying for the second part of the meeting had some food delivered and they said that we can grab some.

De'Andre:

I am definitely grabbing something because man, I am hungry. You know what they ordered?

Kandace:

I think they got hibachi from the new spot down the street in the shopping center.

De'Andre:

I am up for that. I saw that place a couple of weeks ago. Now that I get the opportunity, I am going to see if this will become one of our lunch spots.

Kandace:

You got in that meeting and was right in your element. That is the energy that I am used to seeing.

De'Andre:

Maybe all I needed was a kickstart for the normal routine at hand. Now all we have to do is get use to having these meetings and conferences in our own firm.

Kandace:

True facts. Let's grab a quick plate so we can get this meeting started.

De'Andre:

Yes. We have about ten minutes before we set up for the next meeting.

"JANICE & HER CO-WORKERS RETURN FROM LUNCH"

Janice:

That hit the spot. That took care of those hunger pains.

Malaysha:

I feel you. I am stuffed. I don't know why I did this to myself.

Sherise:

The food was good. We must do it again. Janice, we cannot sit here and act like today didn't happen. You need to address this issue. Dominic looked like he could have hurt you.

Janice:

I know Sherise. This time, he really caught me off guard.

Sherise:

This time? How long have he been this aggressive towards you and how many encounters have you two had?

<u>Janice:</u>

To be truthfully honest, I lost count.

<u>Sherise:</u>

So, it was that many times that you lost count? Why are you letting yourself go through this?

<u>Malaysha:</u>

You have to do something because you going to leave us with no choice but to do something ourselves. Once your grandmother sees those marks, you are not going to have any other choice but tell it. The best thing that you can do is have your grandmother there when you tell De'Andre. He seems to be very fond of your grandmother so I seriously doubt that he will trip in front of her.

<u>Janice:</u>

The key is getting the information to my grandmother before talking with De'Andre.

<u>Sherise:</u>

You may need to leave early so you can get home before De'Andre get off.

<u>Janice:</u>

I will do that. I will see you all later.

<u>Everyone:</u>

Take care Janice.

"MEANWHILE AT JANICE HOUSE"

"DOORBELL RINGS"

<u>Yolanda:</u>

Grandma, I got it. It is Lachelle.

Lachelle:

Hey yall.

Mildred:

Lachelle, what are doing here?

Lachelle:

I need to talk to Janice.

Mildred:

She is not here. Is it anything that me or Yolanda can help you with?

Lachelle:

No Grandma. It is something that I need to talk to her about.

Mildred:

Yolanda, I need you to run to the store for me. Here is my little list.

Yolanda:

Ok Grandma. I will be back.

Mildred:

Now Lachelle, what is it that you need? If I was a gambling woman, I would bet that you are here for money. Why is that the case? What do you need money for?

Lachelle:

Ok Grandma. I will keep it real. I haven't received any child support in a minute. I have reported it but it is taking longer than it should be for me to receive anything.

Mildred:

I get that. Coming by here to get money from Janice is not the answer. You need to apply for more assistance. Having five kids, I know it is hard. Janice cannot always bail you out. You need to leave before De'Andre get here. You don't want to create any issues for them.

<u>Lachelle:</u>

I know that he doesn't really care for me. Ok Grandma, I am gone. Janice just pulled up.

<u>Janice:</u>

Cuz, what brings you by?

<u>Lachelle:</u>

Stopping through to see Grandma. Got to catch up with some folks. See you later.

<u>Mildred:</u>

Alright Janice. Before I get started about Lachelle, where did those marks on your arm come from?

<u>Janice:</u>

It is a long story but I will explain to you later. I promise. Once I tell you, I need your help on how to bring it across to De'Andre.

<u>Mildred:</u>

What do you mean?

<u>Janice:</u>

I would just say this because I know De'Andre will be home shortly. These marks came from a conflict with Dominic.

<u>Mildred:</u>

We will discuss about your brother later. Now, in the case of Lachelle, are you still giving her money after the previous conversation we have had?

Janice:

Grandma, it has been a while since the last time that she got money from me.

Mildred:

She must feel that she can still get money out of you. What needs to happen is you telling her to quit coming by unannounced and only when she needs money. I see your husband pulling up. We will talk later.

Janice:

Ok Grandma.

De'Andre:

Hey Janice, hey Mrs. Mildred. I ran into a couple of old college friends that just moved into town. They invited me to play pool with them tonight. One of them are looking for a position in a firm. Do you mind if I go shoot a little pool?

Janice:

No babe. Have a good tie. Me and Grandma will probably check out this movie based on a true story.

De'Andre:

Ok. I won't be out too late. I'm going to have my friend provide me his credentials. I know that he would be a great asset. I see you two later. Hey Babygirl. You have any more bags in the car?

Yolanda:

Just a couple more. I can get them. It seems like you about to head out.

De'Andre:

Ok Babygirl. See you later.

Yolanda:

Ok Dad. See you later. Grandma, I got all your stuff and then some.

Mildred:

Ok baby, thank you.

Yolanda:

You welcome. I am about to head out. Me and Belinda got good seats at a basketball game. See you later.

Janice:

Ok baby. You all have fun.

Mildred:

Now that everyone is gone, how about we get back to our conversation? Let's start with Lachelle first. The easy resolution to that is to quit giving her money. Quit being her enabler. You are the reason that she refuses to try on her own.

Janice:

Grandma, I have spoken with Lachelle and told her that I cannot keep bailing her out each time she gets into a bind. She was mad talking about cousin, I thought you loved me and that we were family. She was like you know that I am trying.

Mildred:

Now, how many times have you heard that story? What efforts have she made to be trying? Like I said, you need to straight cut her off. She does not need to think that she can continue asking for money from you. She didn't blow up on you like Dominic did she?

Janice:

The only thing that she ever did was get a little angry. She had her short-time attitude but nothing that I could not ignore.

Mildred:

So, you saying that she had an attitude if it didn't go her way?

Janice:

Yes, but I never took any stock into anything she said.

Mildred:

The fact that she crossed the line of being disrespectful, she should have been cut off a long time ago. Now, Dominic is my main concern. Those marks are just ridiculous. On average, the police would be involved in this situation.

Janice:

That is true about what you are saying. My main problem is what am I going to do when it comes to talking to De'Andre?

Mildred:

Is this the first time that Dominic has been that aggressive you or have he did it before?

Janice:

This wasn't the first time. I cannot say that he was more or less aggressive than the first or the last time. It is the fact that he has gotten aggressive. Him getting aggressive like that tells me that he has possibly gotten aggressive with the previous women that he was involved with and that is probably the reason why they left him.

<u>Mildred:</u>

It should not have ever happened. I know that there are some things that you cannot control. We will pull it together and figure out how we will handle this. About to turn in. Getting a little sleepy.

<u>Janice:</u>

I am right there with you Grandma. I was going to wait on De'Andre but the sandman has won this battle. I will see you in the morning.

<u>Mildred:</u>

Goodnight baby. See you in the morning.

<u>END OF SCENE 5</u>

SCENE 6 – TROUBLE IN PARADISE:

Janice:

Good morning De'Andre. The smell from the coffee percolating woke me up. We have a new brand of coffee?

De'Andre:

I saw this new brand and wanted to try it. The aroma was what caught my attention.

Janice:

It does smell good.

De'Andre:

I got a big day at work today. Possibly got a chance to secure four big accounts today. If I get them, everything will be smooth sailing from this point on.

Janice:

That is great to hear.

De'Andre:

I do have a couple of things to ask you before I head out. First, what is going on with your cousin Lachelle? I saw her last night.

Janice:

She was where you were at playing pool?

De'Andre:

Not inside the place. I saw here outside as I was leaving. She came up to me asking for me to help her. She claimed that she desperately needed money so she didn't get put out on the street. She also said that she was told by you to ask me because you didn't have it this time. What did she mean that you didn't have it this time?

Janice:

I had helped her years ago with her kids.

De'Andre:

Years ago? That comment didn't sound like years ago. Apparently, there is something that you are not telling me plus it is only obvious that you like keeping secrets or hiding stuff from me. Talking about deceit. Just to think, you would give me a hard time for something that is hard for you to believe. The difference is I am telling you the truth when you are asking me a question.

Janice:

That is not the case. I do not know what Lachelle is talking about.

De'Andre:

So, in other words, your cousin came up to me out of the blue and just ask me for money saying that you didn't have it this time? I must be crazy.

Janice:

Lachelle is just one of those folks that is just greedy for money. If she feels that she can get money out of you, she will try. I have ran into people where she lives at telling me that she owes them money.

De'Andre:

You are just determined to keep whatever secret that you have going on. You must think that I am crazy enough to believe that lie.

Mildred:

Hey you two. We can hear you upstairs.

De'Andre:

Didn't mean to wake you Mrs. Mildred. I am on my way to work. Me and Janice cannot seem to agree on a topic at hand. Before I leave, tell me something. I take it that you do not know how those marks got on your arms?

Janice:

Lifting boxes at work.

De'Andre:

Bye Janice! See you later Mrs. Mildred.

Mildred:

Janice, you have a real mess right now. The worst thing that you could have did was lie to that man.

Janice:

Grandma, I was caught off guard and backed into a corner. I didn't have a plan on how to approach the situation.

Mildred:

So, you figured lying was the only thing that you could come up with? Lying doesn't buy you any time. Lying only compromises the trust that someone has for you. Knowing De'Andre to be a straight shooter, you have just compromised the trust he had for you. The man is smart. He already knows that you were lying by your body language.

Yolanda:

Mom, what is going on?

Belinda:

Mom, where did those marks on your arms come from?

Mildred:

Janice, you need to go ahead and tell them what is going on.

Janice:

Babygirls, your uncle Dominic did this. Before I get into what happened, your dad is extremely pissed off at me big time. It was first about Lachelle approaching him for money and lying to him saying that I told her to go to him because I didn't have it this time. Second, it is the marks but he doesn't know that it was Dominic that did it. I told him that I was lifting boxes at work.

Belinda:

I am at a loss for words.

Yolanda:

I just texted Aunt Myesha and Aunt Rhonda. They are both on their way over her.

Janice:

Why did you do that?

Yolanda:

Mom, I love you. You need them right now. Your sisters will have your back and help you through this. Mom, why didn't you tell us about this with Lachelle or Uncle Dominic? We are use to Lachelle begging for money. When did it come to this point?

Janice:

Your uncle has in some way been like this for a long time. He was the only boy out of the four of us and momma use to baby him.

Mildred:

My daughter did use to baby him.

Yolanda:

That is still no excuse for him to put his hands on you.

Belinda:

Mom, I agree with Yolanda. Dominic is going to reap what he sews.

"DOORBELL RINGS"

Belinda:

Hey Aunt Myesha, Aunt Rhonda, come on in.

Myesha & Rhonda:

Hey family.

Mildred:

Look at you two. Talk to your sister.

Myesha:

Weren't you suppose to go to work today?

Janice:

I called in today. I told my co-workers that I would be in tomorrow.

Myesha:

Now sis, what is going on? My niece tells me that our brother has a problem keeping his hands off of women. Even worse, De'Andre doesn't know. Janice, why didn't you tell him?

Janice:

He would have probably lost his cool and no telling what he would have done or how he would have reacted.

Rhonda:

With Dominic being our brother, I think his reaction would be different compared to it being a stranger. He would definitely be upset but I don't think it would be as bad as you think. You lying to him, that is a different story.

Janice:

I know. I am going to fix the situation one way or another. It is not going to be an easy task but it has to get done.

Mildred:

Let's go out and get some lunch and come back to help Janice with her approach.

Myesha:

I am with it.

"EVERYONE DEPARTS FOR LUNCH"

"MEANWHILE AT THE FIRM"

Kandace:

De'Andre, I am ordering something for lunch. Is there anything that you have in mind?

De'Andre:

Anything is fine with me. I am not all that hungry.

Kandace:

Really! We have been in meetings back-to-back and I am starving. You say that you are not hungry. What is really going on?

De'Andre:

Nothing. Just focusing on getting these other accounts. We will almost have majority of the accounts in our region.

Kandace:

That is true. I am with you all the way. I have known you for many years and I know that you are not yourself. I won't pressure you. I will place a food order online so we can look over and verify a lot of these financial statements to make sure that they are all accurate.

De'Andre:

Ok. I am looking at this one account and their financial assets are all over the place.

Kandace:

That company was bought out and there are some assets that are being liquidated to settle some debt. They also want to re-invest what they may have afterwards and use it as collateral as well. They have no capital but they feel that any assets that come from this will make a decent return.

De'Andre:

So that explains everything.

Kandace:

Ok De'Andre. What is going on with you? I broke down something that you would have been able to answer standing on your head. You would have gotten this before the question would have finished being asked.

De'Andre:

I do have a lot on my mind. I will start off with Janice lying to me. Her cousin Lachelle came up to me outside of the place me and my college friends were playing pool at asking me for money. She tells me that Janice told her to ask me because Janice didn't have it this time. When I asked Janice what was she talking about, she caught amnesia stating that she didn't know what she was talking about. I then asked her about the marks that were on her arms. She told me that she was lifting boxes at work. You can tell by the marks that they do not appear from lifting boxes at work.

<u>Kandace:</u>

Oh my God. I am so sorry about that. Why do you feel that she had to lie about her cousin and the marks on her arms?

<u>De'Andre:</u>

I don't know but it doesn't sit well with me that she would tell me a bold-faced lie. That only lets me know that she is hiding something.

<u>Kandace:</u>

At least give it some thought before jumping to conclusions. I am not advocating lying but at least try and get to the bottom of what is really going on.

<u>De'Andre:</u>

You have a point. I will give it a lot of thought.

<u>Kandace:</u>

Besides, I don't think Janice is trying to lose a good man. I know she has to think about how long you two have been together. A great provider for his family, she is not crazy to jeopardize that. I tell you what, she is a lucky woman.

<u>De'Andre:</u>

Thank you Kandace. It is always very nice to hear compliments.

<u>Kandace:</u>

You are welcome. Let's get this meeting out of the way so we will be done for the day.

<u>De'Andre:</u>

That will work for me. That will keep my mind on something more constructive.

"DE'ANDRE AND KANDACE GOES INTO THE MEETING"

"JANICE & THE FAMILY RETURNED FROM LUNCH"

Myesha:

Everything was good. We must do that again.

Rhonda:

This is something that I can see us doing once a month. It doesn't have to always be lunch. Any meal will do.

Mildred:

Count me in. That was a nice gathering. Now Janice, what is your game plan?

Janice:

I am going to have to come out with it. I cannot let it drag on because it is only going to get worse.

Rhonda:

Do you need us to be around when you tell him?

Janice:

No. I need to do this by myself. I don't want anyone to be entangled in any of this because I created this.

Myesha:

I hope and pray that he can easily forgive and understand. Being together as long as you two have been is a blessing in itself.

Mildred:

That is so true. Janice, no matter how bad your issue at the time may be, it is never good to be deceptive because it will definitely damage any existing trust. When you have a person that invest so much financially and emotionally, they are looking for a good return because they have made what they have invested so much in their lives. You all are what he lives and work so hard for. I know that you are a loving and caring person. You are also a giving person but I think some of your giving has gotten the best of you. Basically, the giving to your cousin and your brother has gotten you in a position of seeing no return and also not being appreciated. You giving to them has indirectly impacted on you and De'Andre.

Janice:

Everything you all are saying make so much sense and I totally agree. My biggest concern is where his mindset may be at.

Yolanda:

Mom, do you want me and Belinda to talk to him to kind of get a feel of what his mood may be? We won't tell him what you two are going to discuss. We would just kind of fill him out for you.

Janice:

You two do not have to do that. Even if he is in a good mood, I can see it changing once we have our conversation.

Mildred:

If at all by any chance that he gets extremely upset, the best thing for you to do is listen to what he has to say and plus be humble.

Janice:

You right Grandma. If I only knew what was on his mind and what his approach going to be.

Mildred:

You are just going to have to prepare for the unexpected. Just imagine if the shoe was on the other foot, what would you say and how would you approach him? He would know that you would be upset because of not only him hiding stuff from you, but also because he straight out lied to you. If that was the case, that would be your reaction which would be typical, your emotions got in the way trying to protect the wrong family. Your husband is your primary concern. You have to start with your family first.

<u>Janice:</u>

I never thought this would create a big situation.

<u>Mildred:</u>

You have to look at it like this. The people you were helping wasn't no way concerned about you and could care less if you were in some predicament. They figured that you were a gold mine and you just had it to give. That is why they made no effort to pay you back.

"DOORBELL RINGS"

<u>Belinda:</u>

Mom, it is uncle Dominic.

<u>Mildred:</u>

Let him in, please!!!

<u>Dominic:</u>

Hey everybody.

<u>Janice:</u>

What are you doing here? You have a lot of nerve.

<u>Dominic:</u>

I came to apologize because I was wrong for what I did.

<u>Yolanda:</u>

Unk, you really were trippin to put your hands on my mother.

<u>Janice:</u>

Now that you apologized, you have to get out.

<u>Dominic:</u>

Sis, I promise that it will not happen again.

<u>Mildred:</u>

Leave Dominic.

<u>Dominic:</u>

Ok, I am leaving. Sis, I just want to make it right with you. I asked to please forgive me because I was totally wrong.

<u>Janice:</u>

Ok. Dominic, you made your point and you are forgiven. Now you have to leave.

<u>Dominic:</u>

Grandma, I truly am sorry for what I did.

<u>Mildred:</u>

Dominic, you have to leave like she said. She already forgave you. She needs time to herself gather her thoughts on what happened.

<u>Dominic:</u>

Ok. Bye everyone.

<u>Mildred:</u>

Someone peep through the blinds and make sure that he is leaving. Oh my God, he is hard-headed.

Yolanda:

He just got in a read car with someone. They just pulled off.

Mildred:

Janice, to keep him from just popping up on you. I know he is your brother but you may have to get a restraining order.

Janice:

Grandma, do you really think that is necessary? You think that I would have to take it to that point?

Mildred:

Yes, because people are unpredictable and you never know what makes them tick. Your brother grabbing you was unpredictable unless it has become very predictable to you.

Janice:

I understand Grandma. I will take that into serious consideration.

Mildred:

Me and your daughters are going to hit the mall and the movies to give you and De'Andre some time to talk. As a matter of fact, I see him pulling up in the driveway now. Girls, are you ready?

Belinda:

We are almost ready.

De'Andre:

Hey everyone. Long day at work today. I know that I am beat.

Mildred:

Hey De'Andre. Baby, you look tired. I know taken on your own business takes a lot of your time.

De'Andre:

Yes, it does Mrs. Mildred. I plan on taking off in a month or so for about a week or two.

Yolanda:

Hey Dad, I thought I heard you down here. Ready Grandma, we about to head out. Come on Belinda.

Belinda:

Hey Dad. I am ready when you are Grandma.

Mildred:

I am ready. Let's hurry so we can catch these sales.

De'Andre:

Where are you all headed?

Yolanda:

We hitting the mall first and catching a movie afterwards.

Janice:

You all have fun.

De'Andre:

Take care, see you all later.

Mildred, Yolanda & Belinda:

Bye. See you two later.

De'Andre:

Now that everyone is gone, do you want to continue our conversation from where we left off?

Janice:

Yes, we can. What I remember first was we were talking about Lachelle. I had been helping her out.

De'Andre:

So, in other words, I was not hallucinating when she said you told her to come to me for money? You have been supporting a grown woman who doesn't want to work for it herself?

Janice:

She was struggling and needed help with her kids. She was trying to feed them but had no money. I didn't want to see the kids go hungry.

De'Andre:

So let me get this straight. You have this grown woman having all of these kids and it becomes your responsibility to provide support? What about the kid's daddy? Are they all by the same guy? Whom the daddy or daddies are is not important to me at all. The real problem is that you are taking finances out of the household to support something that is no benefit to us. It is not fair to me that I am giving my all for all of us when you are being an atm for others. That probably also explains the marks on your arms.

Janice:

No. The marks are a different story in itself.

De'Andre:

I take that it didn't have anything to do with lifting boxes at your job? By the way, I can recall that she said that she needed the money desperately so she didn't get put out of her place.

Janice:

I don't know anything about her being put out. The only thing she ever tell me is that she needs to feed her kids.

De'Andre:

Whatever her story is, as long as she was getting money, that is all that matters. I believe that you have giving her money for a long time. What is up with the past due bills that I came across in the mail? So, you have been giving her money that you should have been paying your bills with. Now you have something else to tell me as well. Tell me where those marks came from and this time, tell me the truth.

Janice:

The marks came from my brother.

De'Andre:

What the hell you mean they came from your brother? What in the world was going on? So, I take it that he put his hands on you? What is it that you can possibly tell me to keep me from laying hands on him?

Janice:

I am taking a restraining order out on him.

De'Andre:

That does what for me? The fact that you lied to me from the beginning does not make things any better. I am done talking.

Janice:

Where are you going? Wait a minute. I am sorry.

"DOORBELL RINGS"

De'Andre:

It's Felicia and Tianna.

Felicia & Tianna:

Hey De'Andre, hey Janice.

<u>De'Andre:</u>

Hey you two. You two take care. Heading out for a little bit.

<u>Felicia & Tianna:</u>

Take care.

<u>Janice:</u>

Come on in. What's going on with you two? What yall about to get into?

<u>Felicia:</u>

We were coming by to see you. We had not seen you in a minute. The question at hand, is everything good with you? De'Andre looked a little pissed off. Did we come at a bad time?

<u>Tianna:</u>

Janice, what happened? First time I seen De'Andre like this.

<u>Janice:</u>

I have created a mess by trying to help family. I really learned the hard way.

<u>Felicia:</u>

Girl, what happened to your arms? Did De'Andre do this?

<u>Janice:</u>

No he didn't, but how the marks got here is one of the reasons that he is pissed off.

<u>Tianna:</u>

All that matters is that he knows. Why he is so pissed baffles me.

<u>Janice:</u>

It is not the fact that he knows what pissed him off, it is the fact that he didn't know before because I didn't tell him the truth. The marks were not the only thing that he was pissed off about. He found out that I was basically supporting a grown woman. It made the situation worse when he found out that I was so behind in my bills.

Tianna:

Janice, what were you thinking?

Janice:

I froze up because I didn't want him mad at me. I put trust in my family that they would come through and realized that I should have used my better judgment.

Felicia:

It was probably best that he left to go blow off a little steam.

Tianna:

Janice, I don't know what it is going to take to come back from this but I will be praying for you.

Janice:

Thank you girl. I truly appreciate it.

Tianna:

Look like someone is pulling up.

Janice:

That's my grandmother and my daughters. They were hanging out so me and De'Andre could talk.

Felicia:

Well, we won't hand around too long. I have to stop by the store before I head home.

Janice:

Where is your car?

Felicia:

It is over Tianna's house. I rode here with her.

Mildred, Yolanda & Belinda:

Hey everyone.

Felicia:

Hey good people.

Tianna:

Hey now. We came over to see our girl since we haven't seen her in a minute. Definitely had to catch up with her.

Mildred:

Good to see both of you. Me and my grandbabies had a good time out. I know I am going to do this again with them.

Felicia:

I do not blame you Mrs. Mildred. I need a day out myself.

Tianna:

I know what you mean. You ready to head out. Janice, we will catch up with soon. See you all later.

Felicia:

You all take care.

Mildred, Janice, Yolanda & Belinda:

See you later.

Mildred:

Janice, where is De'Andre?

Janice:

Grandma, he left out pissed off at me. I don't know where he went or how long he will be gone.

Yolanda:

So, he didn't say anything? Do you want me and Belinda to go look for him?

Janice:

He didn't say one word. You two do not need to go on a search party.

Mildred:

Right now, maybe the only thing that you can do is give him a little time because this issue is fresh in his mind and on his heart.

Janice:

After all the years that we have been together, our disagreements have never gotten this bad or to this level. There were times that we would go a few minutes or even maybe a few hours without talking. This right here with him leaving home is very unpredictable. Like now, I do not know where he is. It is getting late and he could be anywhere.

Yolanda:

Mom, do not start thinking negatively. I already know where you are going with this. He is not with Kandace.

Janice:

I never said that he was with her. I am just saying that I don't know where he is and it is getting late.

Mildred:

I am willing to bet that he is at one of two places. He is either over his brother's house or his sister's house.

Janice:

Grandma, how can you be so sure?

Mildred:

Janice, he is only upset with you. I seriously doubt that he is out looking for revenge. The love that he has for both of his daughters, I know that he would not want anyone treating them any kind of way. You have to give him the benefit of the doubt. He has never cheated on you. Remember years ago, you thought he cheated and he took a lie detector test willingly and passed with flying colors. Average person would have probably left but he didn't. He also put it behind him like it never happened. That man loves you.

Belinda:

Mom, she is telling you the truth. I would not even bring up the fact that you think he is cheating. That may escalate the fact that he is already pissed and you do not need anything to add to that.

Janice:

I won't bring it up but it would make me feel more comfortable to know where he is at. I got to get some sleep. I got to work tomorrow.

Mildred:

Janice, you better get you some rest. I think Yolanda texted him to see where he was.

Janice:

I am about to go to bed. I will see you all in the morning on my way to work.

Mildred:

Alright baby. Goodnight.

"THE NIGHT COMES TO AN END"

"THE NEXT MORNING"

Mildred:

Good morning Janice.

Janice:

Good morning Grandma. I see you up early this morning.

Mildred:

I figured that I would get some breakfast going so you can get something in your system before going to work.

Janice:

Grandma, that is so thoughtful. It definitely helps me so I don't have to rush to this little spot around the corner from the job before going in.

Mildred:

You still haven't heard from De'Andre?

Janice:

No. Surprised that he didn't come home.

Mildred:

My guess would be over his brother's or sister's house. When Yolanda come down, I will ask her have she heard from him.

Janice:

Ok. I am about to leave. I will talk to you later.

Mildred:

Ok baby. You take care.

Yolanda:

Grandma, was that mom leaving?

Mildred:

Yes, that was her. She is on her way to work. Is Belinda awake? I made breakfast. Also, have you heard from your dad.

Yolanda:

No, I have not heard from him. She is in the shower. I have to ask you something. What do you think about this situation with my mom and dad? Me and Belinda were talking about it and was wondering what was on our mother's mind. I think that their issue could have truly been avoided.

Mildred:

Your parent's situation is no different than any couple that have problems throughout their marriages. One of the major problems with marriages is communication with finances coming right behind that. Something that could be simply fixed can turn into a disaster really quick. What your mom did isn't any different than anybody doing something for a family member. You have to remember when you are committed, you have to know who your family is. She should have discussed that with him if she wanted to help someone. There is a chance that he could have said no or disagree with what she wanted to do. At least he would not feel betrayed.

"MEANWHILE AT JANICE JOB"

Janice:

Hey there good people.

Malaysha:

Hey Janice, how is everything going?

Janice:

Everything is as good as it is going to get.

Sherise:

Hey girl. So, you are saying that something is wrong.

Janice:

To sum it up without sugar-coating, De'Andre left the house last night pissed off at me. He didn't come home last night.

Malaysha:

Are you kidding me? What did you do to make him that upset?

Janice:

He ran into my cousin Lachelle and she approached him asking for money. She told him that I told her to get if from him since I didn't have it. She lied to him about me telling her to ask for it. He didn't believe me because he saw some bills that I was behind on. Also, the marks on my arms, I told him it came from lifting boxes here at work before telling him that my brother did it.

Sherise:

Janice, why did you do that? You just dug a deep hole.

Jermaine:

Are you going to be ok? You know you are like a sister to me.

Janice:

I'm ok. I just have to fix what I created. The problem still is I do not know where he went last night.

Sherise:

Where do you think he went?

Janice:

I do not know but my family told me to give him the benefit of the doubt and not jump to any conclusions.

Malaysha:

How can you not jump to conclusions? He left the house and his whereabouts are unknown. Anything is possible. You don't think he is with his co-worker, do you?

Janice:

No, I don't think he is with her.

Sherise:

How can you be so sure?

Janice:

My grandmother reminded me of something that took place years ago that I had never told you all. A long time ago, I thought De'Andre cheated on me. He took a polygraph test willingly and passed with flying colors. He never threw it back up in my face. He put it behind him like it never happened. He could have left me then but he didn't.

Sherise:

Well, that is definitely justification that he not only he had nothing to hide, he proved that he truly loves you.

Malaysha:

There are not many men that would do what he did. That is a good man right there. Janice, do whatever you need to do to make everything work.

Janice:

Believe me, I am. I just got a text from my daughter Yolanda. She said De'Andre is at home. She said that he just got there about five minutes ago.

Malaysha:

You should leave early and go talk to your husband.

Janice:

I am going to do that. I have to know where he was last night. You all take care.

Sherise, Malaysha & Jermaine:

See you later.

"DE'ANDRE ARRIVES HOME"

De'Andre:

Hey Mrs. Mildred.

Mildred:

Hey De'Andre. Where were you? We were worried.

De'Andre:

I stayed at my brother's house. I had to clear my head.

Mildred:

I am glad that you are ok.

Yolanda:

Hey Dad. Are you ok?

De'Andre:

I am doing ok. Me and your mom has some serious talking to do. I can deal with anything other than someone being very deceitful.

Yolanda:

Dad, I understand where you are coming from. I just hope and pray that you two can work this out.

Mildred:

I hope so too. I know that you are a good man. I know that my granddaughter is a good woman. She makes mistakes and I know with time, she will learn a lot from the mistakes she has made.

De'Andre:

I feel that we can work it out. She just needs to be up front with the truth when a conversation takes place. I have always been up front with her. Speaking of her, she is walking up the walkway.

Yolanda:

Let me open this door. Hey mom.

Janice:

Hey Yolanda.

Mildred:

Hey baby. I see you home early.

Janice:

I decided to leave early. De'Andre, where were you huh? You left and didn't say anything. Were you with Kandace?

Mildred:

Janice! First of all, calm down. Don't go at him like that.

De'Andre:

That's ok Mrs. Mildred. This is why we need marriage counseling. She doesn't know how to talk to anyone. Let me just put it out there. When no one is around, the conversations are sometimes worse. This is the reason that I really don't say much. I am going to get some of my things and go back to where I was.

<u>Janice:</u>

Wait! Where were you?

<u>Mildred:</u>

Janice, calm down. Baby, you were wrong. You should not have gone at him like that. Accusing him of Kandace was a low blow because you were acting out of anger. Just to let you know, he stayed over his brother's house which is where he is going back to.

<u>Janice:</u>

How do we know if that is true?

<u>Mildred:</u>

I guess we don't know for sure if it is true. You have to ask yourself, what is the reason that he is so upset with you? I seriously doubt that he is lying. Remember what he did for you before when you thought that he was cheating.

<u>De'Andre:</u>

Mrs. Mildred, I will talk with you later. Yolanda, take care Babygirl.

<u>Janice:</u>

De'Andre, wait!!!

<u>De'Andre:</u>

I am done talking to you.

<u>Janice:</u>

He left out again Grandma. What am I going to do?

<u>Mildred:</u>

You two are going to have to go to marriage counseling. Talking to a professional will help you get back to the principles.

Janice:

Did you ever have to go to marriage counseling?

Mildred:

Back then, we didn't go because it was not displayed as a helping tool like it is now. There are a variety of benefits to seeking the counseling.

Janice:

I wouldn't know what to say or really know how I would go about it. I think talking to a stranger is what makes me hesitate.

Mildred:

Trust me, a stranger is the best individual that you would need because there would be no biases. Back then, we used to go to older people in the family. That was a bad choice because it gave people a chance to form their own opinion and possibly take a dislike towards the one you are trying to make it work with. Indirectly, you are dealing with that right now.

Janice:

How is that so?

Mildred:

Take your cousin and your brother for instance. They did not come through for you like you thought they would. They did not care about the outcome that you were going to face. In their case, it really didn't have anything to do with your husband literally. It had everything to do with them not having any regards for you. Unfortunately, the situation manifested to affecting your marriage. The counselor would help guide you through what to do and what not to do.

Janice:

I see what you are saying. I guess it would definitely be for the best.

Mildred:

I have a friend that knows a lady that has helped many people in the community. She has helped her and her husband a great deal. I can get in touch with her. The lady's name is Cheryl Wallace. She has over twenty-five years of experience in the profession of marriage counseling. I can reach out to my friend today to give her a call.

Janice:

Ok cool. I am looking forward to starting a new chapter. I know that my marriage is worth everything to me.

END OF SCENE 6

SCENE 7 – RESTORING WHAT IS IMPORTANT:

"VISIT TO THE MARRIAGE COUNSELOR"

Cheryl:

(Buzzes her secretary) Send Mrs. Jones in please.

Janice:

Hello Mrs. Wallace

Cheryl:

Hello Mrs. Jones. Please, call me Cheryl. I love to create a comfortable and relaxing environment.

Janice:

Ok cool. Please call me Janice.

Cheryl:

Gotcha. I know that we have a few minutes while waiting on your husband. Tell me a little about your family, where you work, hobbies, the whole nine yards.

Janice:

I have been married for twenty-five years. We have two daughters. Their names are Yolanda and Belinda and they are both in college. Yolanda is a senior and Belinda is a sophomore. I am a Human Resource Specialist in the private sector. I don't really have much of a hobby. I relax as much as I can. De'Andre just started his own CPA firm.

Cheryl:

That is pretty amazing. (Secretary buzzes Mrs. Wallace. Mr. Jones has arrived. Cheryl responds send him in.)

De'Andre:

Hello Mrs. Wallace

Cheryl:

Please, call me Cheryl.

De'Andre:

Please, call me De'Andre.

Cheryl:

Ok cool. I was just speaking with Janice about the family saying you two have two daughters in college and you started your own CPA firm. Congratulations on all your two's success.

De'Andre & Janice:

Thank you.

Cheryl:

Ok we can get started. Before we began, I wanted to let you two know that I will not base any information provided to me from a bias perspective. I will be open to both parties throughout every step of the progress we are pushing for. I will have a series of questions under the concepts of marriage counseling to see where both of you stand. Before I start off with any questions, I will get a little bit from the both of you. I want to first get your input on what brought you here. I will start off with Janice.

Janice:

Our reasoning for coming in today is to help us out and find out where our connection is and why it was lost.

Cheryl:

Well De'Andre, what would you say brought you here?

De'Andre:

We do not seem like a couple. There is a major disconnect, especially when it comes to communicating. Lately, it seems like I have been kept in the dark about a lot.

Cheryl:

Janice, you say that the connection was lost and De'Andre said that there is a disconnect with communication. So, it would be safe to say that the communication piece is ineffective?

Janice:

To sum it up, I will say that it would be accurate.

Cheryl:

One of the main questions that I get quite much feedback in, are there any serious issues when it comes to trusting one another?

De'Andre:

Trust is one of the major issues but I know that it is much more of an issue for her than it is for me. My main issue is her lying to me unnecessarily because she is hiding things that she is doing for her family. Of course, it is an issue with finances not used in the home. Her main issue for me is her insecurity. I don't know what sparks if off but it is hit or miss on how extreme it is going to be.

Cheryl:

Janice, is what he saying pretty much accurate?

Janice:

Well, I can say that I have helped family members that say they were going to pay me back. As far as the insecurity, I don't think it is that bad. I think that I have gotten much better.

De'Andre:

You don't think it is that bad? How many times have you accused me of cheating? Did I or did I not take a polygraph for you to make you feel comfortable and plus I passed with flying colors?

Cheryl:

Janice, is all of this true?

Janice:

I am afraid that it is. When I feel that I cannot get his undivided attention, someone else has his interest.

Cheryl:

Have you ever tried talking without so much negative energy? What I mean by that is when you are feeling a certain way, must everything you feel have some type of negative result? If you block every opportunity to trust, then nothing will work. The goal is to work on striving for any and everything positive.

Janice:

I do understand that. I guess I would have to try and look at everything as if the shoe was on the other foot.

Cheryl:

You have to have an open mind when it comes to feeling a certain way. If you treat someone wrong, how would you feel if you were treated the same way? How often do you two have a date night?

De'Andre:

To be truthfully honest, I know it has been a while. I know since I have been working on getting my business off the ground, it has been almost two years.

Cheryl:

That is a long time. I know that starting a business is very time consuming, but you two have to find time for yourselves. That is very important because it is an avenue to continue getting to know each other. As time goes on, people change. There is nothing wrong with setting a tone of doing something for the very first time. It will almost be like a first date all over again. Set a date night and explore different things that you have never thought of.

Janice:

I think that is a great idea. I am willing to try anything if it is going to make some progress in improving the things that we need to work on.

Cheryl:

That is great. What about you De'Andre? We are not looking for an overnight result. We have to take baby steps.

De'Andre:

I am willing to do anything necessary. I am not expecting perfection but hopefully see some progress. I am not going to be petty but I also hope that we can talk and share what we are feeling as long as there is an open mind on both sides equally. If each of us have something to say, neither one of us should not be quick to judge or we will be back where we started.

Cheryl:

That sounds fair enough. You two can always ask an opinion of someone else before doing or saying some to get an outside perspective.

Janice:

So, we can get an opinion by letting someone know what I am dealing with?

Cheryl:

No, that is not what I am saying. You can approach someone from a hypothetical perspective.

Janice:

Ok, I get what you are saying. It is one of those what would you do in this situation.

Cheryl:

Exactly. Sometimes people on the outside can give you some of the best advice because they could tell you stuff that you may say I would have never thought of that.

De'Andre:

I agree with you. I have older aunts and uncles that I hear every so often get into conversations about their spouses and how long they have been together. They have talked about their ups and downs, but the key was what kept them together.

Cheryl:

I have a couple of topics to cover before we call it quits for today. DO you two have any friends that are really not mutual that either of you don't care for? It would be one of those friends that you would not miss if they did not come around as often as they did.

Janice:

I cannot say that I do because De'Andre never said anything to me about anyone unless there is someone that I do not know about.

De'Andre:

There was one that I didn't consider to be a major problem but I knew she was a little firecracker. She was a friend of hers that I met at our wedding. She was the one that wished us marital bliss with a detection of sarcasm in her undertone.

Cheryl:

Janice, do you recall who this individual is?

Janice:

He was talking about my friend Pauline. She was divorced twice. She was extremely bitter and thought that everyone's husband was somewhat like both of her exes and it would be a matter of time before we found out. She stopped talking to me along with two of my other friends. They also told me that Pauline distanced herself from them as well. We ran into Pauline's daughter later down the line and asked her how was her mother doing. Pauline's daughter said that she was ok and the reason why she wasn't talking to us anymore.

Cheryl:

What was the reason?

Janice:

Pauline's daughter said to sum it up, no matter what her excuse was, she was determined that she wasn't going to watch all of our marriages fail because of what she went through. In a nutshell from Pauline's daughter, she was jealous.

De'Andre:

I never knew that they stop talking. It must have happened a few years after we were married because I did see her a few times after. Again, I would not say that she was a damper but it would not bother me if she was not around.

Cheryl:

Gotcha. What about you Janice? Is there anyone that you can think of?

Janice:

To be truthfully honest, not really. De'Andre does not have a big circle that is always around. He has a couple of friends that is with their families most of the time when we see them. I will admit, he doesn't like drama so when he feels that he is around it, he completely separates himself from it.

Cheryl:

That is great knowing he is all about protecting the best interest in both of you. My next question and last for today so we can wrap it up until the next visit, what do you thing brings on the insecurity urge?

Janice:

I have been hurt badly before I met De'Andre. I thank God that I never caught anything. I revisit that moment when De'Andre is spending a lot of time at work.

Cheryl:

Do you think that De'Andre is cheating?

Janice:

Sometimes it gets harder to not think that way with us not spending a lot of time together. Sometimes I think he rather be at work more than at home.

Cheryl:

De'Andre, what do you think about the statement she just made?

De'Andre:

First off, I would like to say that the time that we are not together goes parallel with work. I didn't always spend a lot of time at work. When it came to putting a business together, that is where the time went. Now, she has accused me of cheating on numerous occasions. No matter how much I have tried convincing her otherwise, once her mind is set that is it. She has accused me of my now business partner that she has conversed and hung out with. After taking a polygraph prior to prove to her after passing with flying colors would satisfy her insecurity issue, but apparently it hasn't done a thing.

Cheryl:

How does it make you feel after everything you have did to try and prove your love for her?

De'Andre:

I felt neglected like I was not benefitting in this marriage. The fact that I am upfront and forthcoming with her, I do not get the same from her she was quick to accuse me of something but also consistent in being deceitful. The bad part about it is once she got caught in her deceit, she would try making an excuse for what she is trying to hide. Sometimes I feel when she is accusing me, I get that feeling she is hiding something. Prime example, when I ran into her cousin that asked me for money, she accused me of my business partner a couple of days prior.

Cheryl:

Janice, is this true?

Janice:

I have accused him because his business partner thinks highly of him. My cousin has gone to him asking for money and told him that I said to give it to her because I didn't have it that specific time. I had been helping her out before.

Cheryl:

I take it that De'Andre didn't know?

Janice:

No, he didn't.

Cheryl:

We will stop right here and continue where we are leaving off with. I can schedule for a session next Wednesday if that works for the both of you?

De'Andre:

That works for me. Can we go for Wednesday morning? I have a meeting and do not have to be there until noon.

Janice:

That should work for me as well.

Cheryl:

Ok. You two will be my first appointment at eight in the morning.

De'Andre:

Ok. I will see you then.

Janice:

I will be there. De'Andre, I am going home. Where are you going?

De'Andre:

I am going to work. I have a couple of meetings today. Afterwards, I will be going to my brother's house to stay.

Janice:

Oh really? It's like that?

De'Andre:

I think we have to give ourselves a little space to be able to analyze everything and make necessary changes towards improvement on both of us. I do not want to constantly get scrutinized about the littlest thing.

Janice:

So, I take it that going to your brother's house is the solution?

De'Andre:

No, that is not what I was saying. You are so quick to jump to conclusions. I have to get to this meeting. I will come to the house so we can talk more.

Janice:

I don't want you to trouble yourself.

De'Andre:

Bye Janice. That wasn't even necessary.

"DE'ANDRE HEADS TO WORK"

"JANICE HEADS HOME"

"JANICE ARRIVES HOME"

Janice:

Hey, is anyone home?

Mildred:

I am here Janice. I am the only one here.

Janice:

Good. It gives us a chance to talk.

Mildred:

Ok Babygirl. I am all ears. What's going on?

Janice:

We went to the counseling session and I must say that it is helpful. It kind of opened my mind up to quite much. It kind of let me know about me.

Mildred:

What do you mean when you say that?

Janice:

Hearing things from her perspective almost as if she was speaking to me through him. She gave us some advice on going back to the very beginning when we were dating. She said that we should set up date nights. I do agree with her. I did do one thing wrong after we left. I went at him wrong not acknowledging how he may have been feeling. My emotions got int the way and it wasn't so much of just what I said but it was also how I said it. I know that is something that I have to work on.

<u>Mildred:</u>

Acknowledging what you did wrong is truly commendable. Saying it to him will definitely be more effective than saying it to me. You were able to tell me with such ease because we talk to each other on a regular basis. You need to display that same energy to him as well.

<u>Janice:</u>

I get what you are saying Grandma. Right now, De'Andre is a little heated at me and he said that he will be staying at his brother's house for a little bit.

<u>Mildred:</u>

Janice, you have to keep in mind that when you react emotionally on how you feel, the person's reaction may not be what you expect. You cannot expect De'Andre to react in a way you feel he should react because he is not going to know what you are thinking. Baby, it is called a difference of opinion. If you were to base everything on how you see things the way it needs to be, there would not be any imperfection and you know that there is no one in the world that is perfect. If he does something or responds a certain way and you are getting mad, yes you are wrong.

<u>Janice:</u>

I understand what you are saying Grandma. I just hope that I am not pushing so hard to the point that he gets so disgusted with me. I know that

I can be hard to deal with. I will admit that my main issue is my insecurity. I cannot help the fact that Kandace gets to me. Grandma, I cannot help it. She is a beautiful woman that is around my husband the majority of the day.

Mildred:

First, you have to get over the insecurity about Kandace. You cannot hold that against your husband. He is a good man so you have nothing to worry about.

"MEANWHILE AT THE CPA FIRM"

Kandace:

I think that this meeting went extremely well. We possibly have four more that will be utilizing our services. Pretty soon, we are going to have to expand our business abroad if our growth continues at this pace.

De'Andre:

It did go pretty well. Looking forward to our next meeting.

Kandace:

De'Andre, what is going on? I notice that you haven't been yourself. You didn't really do much talking at the meeting.

De'Andre:

Got a lot on my mind. Me and Janice went to marriage counseling before I came in. She really irritated me because she doesn't get it. I can tell from the facial expression of the counselor that she noticed that not only I was aggravated, but she picked up on what aggravated me. I also brought up the issue about her insecurities and how she was accusing me of being with you.

Kandace:

Wait a minute. She is accusing you of messing with me? Where did this come from?

De'Andre:

Her problem about you is she thinks that you are a beautiful woman and I lost interest in her. I told her that I didn't understand the fact of her not only knowing you but also hanging out with her and my daughters.

Kandace:

De'Andre, I don't know what to say. I would not have ever thought that she felt that way. Was there anything I did to make her feel uncomfortable?

De'Andre:

Kandace, you did not do anything. That is just something that she will have to come to terms with. No one can blame you for anything. Being beautiful is not a crime.

Kandace:

Thank you for the compliment. I cannot recall the last time I received a decent compliment.

De'Andre:

You are more than welcome. Our next meeting should not last as long. I would mind grabbing something to eat before going into the next meeting.

Kandace:

What do you have in mind? I don't want anything heavy.

There is a place about two blocks up the road that sale stuff like flatbreads with various toppings. My favorite is the grilled Italian chicken flatbread.

Kandace:

Sounds good to me. Let's get that order placed. Grilled Italian chicken would be a first for me.

De'Andre:

Trust me, you will not regret it. I am ordering it online. They have delivery as long as it is over a certain amount which I know I will reach.

Kandace:

Ok cool, that will work for me. I'm not trying to get deep in your business, but how is everything going with you and Janice? I ask out of concern for two good people I know.

De'Andre:

No, it is ok. I do not have a problem sharing. Things haven't really been all peachy cream lately. She has been very deceitful. Some stuff as simple as giving money to her family that don't want to earn it themselves. That bad part is seeing some of her bills fall way behind that should have never happened. I have always been taught to always make sure your own home front is taken care of before you do anything else outside of that.

Kandace:

I understand that philosophy all so well. I had that same issue in a prior relationship as well. The guy's cousin got real nasty with me. I cut my losses of that family affair.

De'Andre:

Do you regret it or think about what it could have been if the circumstances were different?

Kandace:

I don't regret anything about my decision. I thought about it a couple of times but chased the thought out of my mind shortly afterwards. I see that the food has arrived. I will grab it.

De'Andre:

Ok.

Kandace:

Everything smells good.

De'Andre:

I know that you will enjoy it. Can I ask you a personal question?

Kandace:

Sure.

De'Andre:

What kind of characteristics do you look for in a man? I ask that question being curious if some of the same attributes apply across the board.

Kandace:

For the most part and also basing it on what some of my closest friends look for, we are all aligned with looking for some of the same qualities. They range from being extremely caring and truthfully upfront.

De'Andre:

Let me ask you this. As long as you have known me, Do I seem to be that caring type of individual? I know you are not around when I am at home but my demeanor and personality is basically the same at all times.

Kandace:

From what I can see other than when you are at home, you are that caring individual that always thin about growth for you and your family. I never see you leave them out of anything. I see how crazy your daughters are about you.

De'Andre:

I wonder what is the disconnection that we are having. If I have always been about my family, then what is the driving force behind her being deceitful? What is the source of the issue that brought us to this point?

Kandace:

The only way to get the answer to that is for her to be upfront and tell it. If someone is being deceitful, not saying it is a good reason but there is a reason why people do it. Our meeting is in a half hour. Let's finish our food so we can get this meeting on the way.

De'Andre:

You right. Time is getting away. Thanks for being that shoulder to lean on. It is great knowing that I can have someone to talk to that not only knows me, but can also be able to help me understand things where I do not see light.

Kandace:

I am always available for a near and dear friend. Knowing you two for as long as I have, I know that your love for each other is definitely worth saving. The meeting is about to start. Let's knock another one out of the park.

"DE'ANDRE & KANDACE GOES INTO THE MEETING"

"MEANWHILE AT JANICE'S JOB"

Malaysha:

Hey Janice, I didn't know that you were coming in today.

Janice:

I decided to come for a half day to get some work done so I do not have to play catch up. Where is everyone?

Malaysha:

Jermaine took off today and Sherise had an appointment that she will be returning from later one. How is everything going?

Janice:

Me and De'Andre just left from a meeting with a marriage counselor.

Malaysha:

Oh really? How was the visit?

Janice:

It was good. She shed a little light on me about some things that I wasn't thinking about plus helped me to have more of an open mind towards other people's feelings. The various issues that me and De'Andre have can easily be worked out but it is totally up to us and how we approach it.

Malaysha:

What do you think is going to be the hardest challenge for you? I know with as long as you two been together, it is definitely worth putting in every effort of saving.

Janice:

I know that one of the hardest challenges is probably having better control of my feelings. I know that I been basically driving him crazy when it comes to my insecurities. Sitting back thinking about it, I know that is part of the reasons arguments are started is because me going through my moment. I used to say, why is he walking away and abruptly ending our conversations. It also sometimes took my daughters to point out where I was wrong for jumping to conclusions. There was also a comment that De'Andre made to me that stuck with me and made me think. He said I was always willing to talk but is really not willing to listen.

Malaysha:

The fact that you can acknowledge what your challenges are, the process should not be as difficult as it could be if no one was willing to admit that there is an issue. If you know that your insecurities are contributing to the existing problem, you definitely have to gain that control. The fact that he is not doing anything to give you any idea that he is cheating is an advantage to you.

<u>Janice:</u>

I agree with everything you are saying.

<u>Sherise:</u>

Hey there you two. Janice, I thought that you were out today?

<u>Janice:</u>

Wanted to catch up on some work and plus it will help take my mind off of me and De'Andre going to a marriage counselor.

<u>Sherise:</u>

Is it working for you? I know that there are no overnight miracles. Is it a step that you are going to stay with?

<u>Janice:</u>

Yes it is. I am going to stay with it because the counselor has provided some insight that was very helpful to fixing the existing problem.

<u>Sherise:</u>

Has the counseling made any changes at home?

<u>Janice:</u>

I would not say it has yet. I will admit that I did go off at him the wrong way when we left. He is at his brother's house for the time being. It was a moment that I had and took the wrong approach. He left to avoid an argument. I want him back home because it is driving me crazy.

Malaysha:

Janice, let me ask you something. Have you ever thought of seeking help outside of counseling?

Janice:

No. What do you suggest?

Malaysha:

I am simply suggesting something that will help you out when you are feeling a certain way. It will be an avenue in which you would have time for yourself.

Sherise:

Janice, I agree with her. It is best that you have an avenue that you can work on yourself. If you do not have that, it will not help you on your issue when it comes to jumping to conclusions.

Janice:

I am willing to do that, especially if it is going to help me and De'Andre.

Malaysha:

At the end of the day, that is all that matters. Strengthening your union back with De'Andre is the ultimate goal.

Janice:

It definitely is. I am going to ask the counselor if she has anyone that can recommend me. It is about that time to get out of here. I will catch you all tomorrow.

Malaysha & Sherise:

See you tomorrow.

"DE'ANDRE & KANDACE DEPARTS MEETING"

De'Andre:

Kandace, I think that we ought to be putting some plans together for expansion. If these meetings keep going at the rate that it is going at, we will soon become one of the biggest firms in our area.

Kandace:

I was thinking the same thing. It is so amazing that our clientele count has increased dramatically. I did not predict growth this quick at all.

De'Andre:

This is that "Dream Come True" feeling you have as a kid. I always wanted to own my own business when I was young. Now the fact that we are here today, it is proof that dreams do come true. We have to set up a meeting with the state board to make sure that we cover everything necessary for expansion.

Kandace:

I am all for that. When I think back to what my dreams were, it was never this. I always wanted to join the military but my dad said that no daughter of mines will be going in the armed forces. He said that I would take on two or three jobs to pay for you to go to college. I can see that it truly paid off. It is a blessing that I will not take for granted.

De'Andre:

I think that once we hit our goal, I am going to buy my dream car. I figure my kids are grown and taken care of.

Kandace:

What is your dream car? Mine is anything or any model Range Rover.

De'Andre:

A Lamborghini Diablo is my dream car. Before I throw that type of money out there, I would rather pay off my house first. I would not get into that type of debt without having a major purchase like a home out of the way. I have colleagues from college that is deep in debt like that.

<u>Kandace:</u>

Definitely a smart move. We are going to reach our goal. I am claiming it. Before you know it, we will be in a magazine as one of the top firms in the country. Now that would be the ultimate goal.

<u>De'Andre:</u>

Yes it will. I am about to head out. Me and my brother are going to catch up with a couple of friends to play some pool. You calling it a night?

<u>Kandace:</u>

Probably going to heat up my leftovers and watch some Netflix. I may also call my sister to see what they are doing. Along with that, I am going to continue to celebrate our continued success in our business. I am taking in all my dreams come true.

<u>De'Andre:</u>

I heard that. I will see you tomorrow.

<u>Kandace:</u>

Take care.

"DE'ANDRE & KANDACE DEPARTS"

"MEANWHILE AT THE JONES HOUSEHOLD"

<u>Janice:</u>

Hey Grandma, how was your day?

<u>Mildred:</u>

Everything was good until I saw your brother and cousin.

Janice:

Did they come by the house?

Mildred:

No. I saw both of them in the grocery store. That is the worst place to run into someone because they know that if you are in the grocery store, you are spending some money.

Janice:

Did anyone of them ask you for any money?

Mildred:

Both of them did. Lachelle tried running game talking about you told her to get it from me. Your brother, on the other hand, he showed no shame and got a little belligerent. I take it that Lachelle had a food stamp card because for her to be shopping and then run into me, she still asked for money. She already had a cart full before I saw her.

Janice:

That is crazy. I am going to have a talk with both of them. First thing that I am going to say is that they need to stop coming to me for money. I am also going to tell Lachelle to quit going to people saying that I told her to go to them. They are part of the problem that I let happen and is one of the reasons to my problem with De'Andre.

Mildred:

You have to keep in mind of the resistance that you are going to get when you talk with them. No matter what the response is, you have to stick to what is more important. Your marriage is your responsibility and it doesn't mean anything to them.

Janice:

That is absolutely true. I know one thing. I have to get De'Andre back home before our next visit to the counselor. The longer that he is staying with his brother, the less progress we will be making.

Mildred:

When you speak with him, you will have to have an open mind and not jump to any conclusions. If that happens, it is going to have you back at square "A".

Janice:

I know Grandma. I have been working on that. I know that was what made him go to his brother's house. This time I won't be so quick to speak but be much quicker to listen.

Mildred:

It is good that you do that because it will at least show him that there is some consideration being shown for his feelings. I bet that he would be very open to talk and come to an agreement. Like I told you before, I know that De'Andre is a good man and it will be worth the fight. Think about your daughters.

Janice:

I will shoot him a text to see if he is available.

Mildred:

That is good. The earlier, the better.

Janice:

I just sent it. I will wait to see if he responds back.

Mildred:

What exactly did you say to him?

Janice:

I asked him if he can come by so we can talk. I told him that it was very important. He just responded and said he will be over in about fifteen minutes. I am going to see if he will stay tonight. I figure if he would do that then he will stay and not go back over to his brother's house. He needs to be here.

Mildred:

Just remember what I said. Keep an open mind. Someone just pulled up.

Janice:

It is Yolanda.

Yolanda:

Hey mom, hey Grandma.

Janice:

Hey baby.

Mildred:

Hey Shug. Where is your sister?

Yolanda:

She is over a friend's house getting her hair done.

Janice:

Have you already eaten?

Yolanda:

No. I am starving. What do you have in mind?

Janice:

Thinking about ordering some from Cameron's restaurant. Haven't gotten anything from them in a while.

Mildred:

I am good with that.

Yolanda:

I am too Grandma. Some soul food would definitely hit the spot.

Janice:

I am going online to place the order before your dad gets here.

Yolanda:

Dad's coming home?

Janice:

Me and him do need to talk.

Yolanda:

Mom, that is good. This is where he needs to be. I know things will work out because I am already claiming it. That looks like dad coming up the walkway. Let me open the door. Hey dad, how are you?

De'Andre:

Hey Babygirl, I am good. Where is your sister?

Yolanda:

She is over her friend's house getting her hair done.

Mildred:

Hey Shug, how are you doing?

De'Andre:

I am good Mrs. Mildred. How have you been?

<u>Mildred:</u>

Everything is good. It is really good to see you. I know that you and my granddaughter need to talk so we will be out of your hair.

<u>Yolanda:</u>

Cameron is walking up. The food is here. Hey Cameron.

<u>Cameron:</u>

Hey there everyone. Thank you for your continuing support of my restaurant.

<u>Janice:</u>

We will not have it any other way.

<u>Mildred:</u>

Shug, you all have some good food coming out of there.

<u>Cameron:</u>

Thank you. Yall take care.

<u>Yolanda:</u>

Man, I am ready to throw down.

<u>Janice:</u>

De'Andre, I ordered us all some food. I hope you are hungry. We can talk after we are done eating if that is ok with you.

<u>De'Andre:</u>

That will be fine. I had not eaten yet so that is perfect.

<u>Mildred:</u>

Everything smells good. Oh my God, you have sock-it-to-me-cake. I know that I am not going to be any good after eating all this food.

Yolanda:

I know that is right Grandma. I know that Belinda is missing out on this right now. I may take a picture and text it to her (lol).

Janice:

Now Yolanda, you know that you are not right. You are going to have that girl speeding across town. If she gets a ticket, you are paying for it (lol).

Mildred:

I am about to get some sock-it-to-me cake and go upstairs.

Yolanda:

I will get these dishes. There is on a few dishes in there that I can knock out really quick.

Janice:

De'Andre, let's go into the living room so we can talk. I figure that we can do a little catching up and hopefully change our current situation.

De'Andre:

I am all ears. What is on your mind?

Janice:

First off, I want to apologize for the way that I came off on you. I will admit that I was wrong on so many levels. I would love for you to return home if that is ok with you. This is where you really need to be. I feel that if you are here, we can work on us.

De'Andre:

I can agree with you on that. There are a lot of things that need to be worked on. First, all these secrets and deception needs to come to an end. I don't understand the point of all of this. Second, your issue about Kandace, I definitely do not understand. You have accused me a number of times of cheating with her. You two used to be really close. The minute you stop talking to her was the time you started thinking that we were messing around.

Janice:

I was very curious because all the time you two were spending at work. When I look at what was accomplished as far as the business, it was very obvious that you were thinking about having more for us. I was very insecure because Kandace is a gorgeous woman with everything going for her. With my husband being around her for most of the day, I figured that you would find some interest. I am pretty sure that she doesn't have any problem getting any guy's attention.

De'Andre:

You have to trust my judgment. Do you think I would have gone into business with her if she was going to be a problem? She wasn't trying to lose any money on her investment just like I wasn't. She is good at what she does. Out of all my colleagues, she is one of the best. The great thing is that we are equal across the board.

Janice:

Well, that is good to know. The great thing is at least we are talking about it.

De'Andre:

That is why communication is a key element necessary in a marriage. When you have a question, there is nothing wrong with asking about something that you are curious about. If you jump to conclusions, then I will shut down.

Janice:

I understand. I promise, I really do. Well, I am about to call it a night. Got to go to work tomorrow. The day after tomorrow, we have a follow up with Cheryl. I took that day off.

De'Andre:

I am available until late afternoon that day. I'm not going in until that afternoon for a conference. I am going in early tomorrow to go to a board meeting. See you in the morning. Goodnight.

"THE NEXT MORNING"

De'Andre:

Good morning everyone. I have breakfast in the kitchen. I am about to head out.

Mildred:

Good morning De'Andre. How sweet of you.

Janice:

Thank you for making breakfast. I am definitely hungry.

Yolanda:

Dad, you save me some money this morning. I was going to stop and grab something.

De'Andre:

Where is your sister?

Yolanda:

She is still sleep. She got in late.

De'Andre:

Oh ok. Well, you all take it easy. About to go get ready for our meeting at work and discuss some of the conference for tomorrow.

Mildred, Janice & Yolanda:

See you later.

Yolanda:

Mom, is dad back home for good?

Janice:

I sure hope so. We talked last night and did not argue once at all.

Yolanda:

That is great.

Mildred:

With him staying last night, you can tell that he wanted to be home. I got that vibe. You would see the signs if he didn't want to be here.

Janice:

I wouldn't really consider myself in the clear just yet. I say that because I created an issue that made him leave the house. We have disagreed many of times but this was the first time that he has left home. Who's to say that it won't be the last.

Mildred:

Baby, you must have faith. Keep your negative thinking out of it. That is where the counseling comes in to play.

Janice:

I know Grandma. I am really starting to recognize some of the downfalls that could have been avoided. It is not so much of thinking negative but accepting responsibility. I truly know that he is a good man, but at times I get a little nervous because of my own personal issues. I know that he has tolerated a whole lot. I know that marriage vows say for better or worse. It does not say let's see how worse you can make it before your spouse decides to leave.

<u>Mildred:</u>

The fact that you two are going to counseling makes everything that much better.

<u>Janice:</u>

It does show us making progress in trying to make things better. I know that I am going to devote all effort necessary to get back to where we were.

<u>Yolanda:</u>

Mom, think about something that you did when you two first got together. Where was the first place you went together that meant so much.

<u>Janice:</u>

I wish we could but it is impossible now. His mom catered a meal for us. It was an elegant seafood meal.

<u>Yolanda:</u>

That is not hard to duplicate. Me, Belinda and Grandma can put something together for you two. We probably cannot get it down pack of what Grandma actually made but I think we can come close.

<u>Janice:</u>

Ok, that will work. We have to sit down and plan it out. I think it will be something that will spark that flame that has withered out.

<u>Mildred:</u>

Janice and Yolanda, I think that is a great idea. I know that De'Andre will appreciate that.

Janice:

Let's plan it. I am about to head out of here so I won't be late to work. See you all later.

Mildred & Yolanda:

Have a good day.

"MEANWHILE AT THE FIRM"

De'Andre:

Kandace, do you have the portfolios for the board meeting?

Kandace:

Yes I do. I got them done early because I knew that this day would sneak up on us quickly. We have time to look over them before the meeting starts. I have all five portfolios. There are three of them already approved to get started. The other two should not be a problem.

De'Andre:

Ok cool. We have a half hour before we start. Man, I tell you. I am glad that we are in a position that we are in. Just to think, we are about to take over the whole region if the progress continues to be very consistent.

Kandace:

I know exactly how you feel. I meant to ask you how were things coming along?

De'Andre:

I actually stayed at home last night. Me and Janice sat up and talked for a good while. I would say that it was the most we communicated in a minute. I did get some points across to her that bothered me.

<u>Kandace:</u>

That is good. At least you two talked about it. Do you two have any more counseling sessions?

<u>De'Andre:</u>

We have one tomorrow morning. Hopefully when we go tomorrow, I am looking for this visit or maybe no more than one more visit would be it.

<u>Kandace:</u>

That will be great. After that many years together, it is definitely worth saving.

<u>De'Andre:</u>

I agree with you. I wish that it would have not ever gotten to this point. I feel that a lot of valuable time was truly wasted. The one thing that I can say is that this step was necessary because without it, this was only going to get worse.

<u>Kandace:</u>

I am happy that you were able to come to terms with Janice on what is important and also be able to look at the time invested. I would just have to say that Janice would have been crazy to let you slip away. Not saying it in a mean way, I am basing it off of what I have witnessed in my own family. I have a couple of aunts who are extremely bitter behind making the wrong choice by listening to the wrong people.

<u>De'Andre:</u>

Thank you Kandace. I feel the same in return by me even letting her slip away. I also agree with you about people making the wrong choices and regretting it because of listening to an influence. Well, we have about ten minutes left before this board meeting. Let's get this step out of the way before the conference tomorrow.

<u>Kandace:</u>

I am ready.

"DE'ANDRE & KANDACE GOES IN BOARD MEETING"

"MEANWHILE AT JANICE'S JOB"

<u>Janice:</u>

Hey everyone.

<u>Sherise:</u>

Hey there Janice.

<u>Malaysha:</u>

Hey there girl. Love the hairstyle. I need to get over there and see Felicia.

<u>Jermaine:</u>

Hey there sis, how have you been?

<u>Janice:</u>

I have been pretty good. I really cannot complain.

<u>Malaysha:</u>

How are things coming along?

<u>Janice:</u>

Things seem to be going in the right direction. We have our next session scheduled tomorrow. With the way things are going, this may be our last session because we been able to talk about what is on our mind without any arguing. Don't get me wrong, we will take the advice from the counselor even if she recommends more sessions.

Malaysha:

That is great. You seemed to be a little bit happier.

Janice:

I will say that I am in a better place with my marriage than before.

Jermaine:

It is good to see true love working through any and everything. Sis, what is the one thing that you wish that you could do over to alleviate any problems that may have come in existence? What toxic situation would you remove all together?

Janice:

The one that I would change is to have more of an open mind and not be so quick to jump to any conclusions. I know that I have been bad with that for years and fortunately De'Andre dealt with an absorbed it for so long. The toxins would be anything that always carry negative perspectives. To sum it up, there are some family members that I really need to distance myself from.

Sherise:

That is always a good thing when you know who creates the trouble, we all have those family members. Most of the time, it is the ones that we are the closest to. Sometimes the hurt feeling is finding out that they never cared for you as much as you thought they did.

Malaysha:

I can definitely attest to that. My cousin that I grew up with was the one that I had my reality check with. We don't talk now because of her funny ways. It doesn't bother me at all. It did before because we were so close.

Janice:

My brother Miguel and my cousin Lachelle are my two main burdens. Once I change up how I deal with them, they probably will stop talking to me anyway. I just have to wrap that around my mind and accept it.

Jermaine:

Trust me sis, it gets easier the quicker you start. The fact that I had to do it, I felt better afterwards. I am not going to lie, it was a hurting feeling but it was truly necessary.

Janice:

I understand exactly where you are coming from. I know that it is going to be hard either way. I know that there are a couple of other family members I know that De'Andre kind of keeps his distance from because they do have quite much drama surrounding their lives. That is one thing that he will quickly separate himself from.

Sherise:

As long as there is drama in existence, there is always going to be a problem in a marriage.

Malaysha:

Janice, keep those folks away. Their ultimate goal is to really destroy what you have. Too much jealousy in the world and most of it is closer to you than you think.

Jermaine:

I agree with her sis. Jealousy is an ugly trait. It destroyed my friendship with a guy that I grew up with. The problem was that I never knew.

Janice:

That is true. I am going to make sure that they all understand.

Malaysha:

Do not focus on being hard on yourself. You have to focus more on making your marriage better and stronger. If you put that first and foremost, you should not ever have any problems. Family members may not like it but your own family are the most important.

Sherise:

True facts spoken from a strong woman.

Janice:

I am not going to mess this up again. It is all my fault that we were in the predicament that we were in. I am glad that I have you all for support. It definitely makes life easier knowing that I have people that I can relate to and relate to me without feeling that I am backed into a corner to figure it out myself. It is truly a blessing.

Malaysha:

That is so true. This is half of my life right here. Don't get me wrong, I do have a social life. The only person that I have to be responsible for is me. Since it is just me, I look forward to coming to work to keep me busy.

Jermaine:

I am right there along with you. I do have a brother and three sisters that all gather together with me once a month at my mother's house. She cooks a big feast for us all.

Sherise:

That is what I am talking about. Let us know the next time you have a family gathering, tell your mom that she just inherited another daughter (lol).

Janice:

I am about to head out a little early. I have to go by the store and pick up some stuff so I can prepare dinner. See you all later.

Sherise, Malaysha & Jermaine:

Bye Janice.

"MEANWHILE AT THE FIRM"

De'Andre:

Man, the board was trying to drive a hard bargain.

Kandace:

Things were a little intense but I am not worried. I think that they wanted to make sure of all our checks and balances.

De'Andre:

At least when it comes to policies and procedures, we always practice what we preach.

Kandace:

Exactly. I know that I would not have it any other way.

De'Andre:

I am glad that we reach the point of where we are not. We definitely came a long way from our very beginning. We climbed a lot of obstacles.

Kandace:

To be truthfully honest, I never thought that I would ever see my name on a business nevertheless affiliated to a firm. I know once my mother saw the start of our business, she was so excited and told all of her friends.

De'Andre:

I only wished that my mom could have physically seen our accomplishments. A long time ago, we sat and talked about plans for my future. I feel that she spoke it into existence. She taught me to keep pushing for what I want because opportunities don't just fall into your lap. I have her drive and motivation.

Kandace:

I know that she would have been proud of the man that you have become. I am sure that she is looking down from the heavens smiling at you.

De'Andre:

I can see her saying that I knew you can do it and I am so proud of you. My sister and brother also inherited her drive as well.

Kandace:

That is great because at least having siblings that are independent and responsible is a plus. I know how some family, especially siblings, can be a problematic issue at times.

De'Andre:

I know what you mean. I know Janice had to deal with this when it comes to her brother Dominic. Well, I'm about to head home. I will be in tomorrow afternoon. I figured after the conference, we may be running the rcgion. I will scc you tomorrow.

Kandace:

Ok, I will see you tomorrow. Take care.

"MEANWHILE AT THE HOUSE"

Belinda:

Hey mom, my sorors and I are having a fundraiser to raise money for the building of living quarters for the homeless. Can you let your co-workers know? We are going to be doing a number of things to raise the money. We are even involving kids' events for them to showcase their talents.

<u>Janice:</u>

I will definitely let them know. I can guarantee that you will receive their support.

<u>Mildred:</u>

I will also let all my friends know. I am pretty sure that they will pass it along to the children and their grandchildren as well. I am always all about helping the community in every way. I see a couple of guys often when I am out and about that I know are homeless.

<u>Belinda:</u>

Grandma, if you can please get their names and where they are at majority of the time. I figure once this project gets off the ground, we may be asked if we know anyone who needs the assistance.

<u>Mildred:</u>

That will not be a problem. I would love to see those two get the help that they need. Knowing that we made a contribution to help those in need is a great feeling in itself. Make sure that you let your dad know so he can tell his fraternity brothers.

<u>Belinda:</u>

He already knows. I texted him earlier today to let him know.

<u>Janice:</u>

Belinda, where is your sister?

<u>Belinda:</u>

She went to the movies with some friends of hers. They were going out afterwards.

<u>Janice:</u>

Oh ok. I bought some chicken that I put in the kitchen. I also have potato salad in there. I didn't feel like cooking plus we have an appointment in the morning with the counselor. With as much progress as we been making, this may be our last visit.

Mildred:

I am going into the kitchen and get something to eat. Here comes De'Andre now. He is pulling up in the driveway now.

Janice:

I am going to eat a little bit of chicken and going to bed.

De'Andre:

Good evening everyone. Man, I am tired. Today was a long day.

Janice:

You even look tired. The board meeting must have been long.

De'Andre:

It was very long. After the conference tomorrow, we will have control over the region.

Mildred:

I am extremely proud of you De'Andre.

De'Andre:

Thank you Mrs. Mildred. I truly appreciate it. I am about to turn in so I can get up early for our appointment.

Mildred:

Ok. Get you some rest. I will see you tomorrow.

Janice:

I am coming right behind you shortly after I eat a little something first.

Mildred:

Janice, I wanted to ask you what would you be looking for it the session tomorrow? Also, if you don't get exactly what you are looking for, will you be patient and continue?

Janice:

Grandma, I am willing to do whatever it takes but I don't totally understand what you are asking.

Mildred:

I am saying that you said things are going great and I believe you. What I am getting at is his feelings are not your feelings and you have to be open to that is all I am saying.

Janice:

Grandma, I do understand and I am open to that. I realized what I have created. From this point since I Know what I should be avoiding, if anyone has a problem with what I do when it comes to my family, the door is right there and they are no longer welcome here.

Mildred:

That was the way I was when it came to your grandfather. We had some very disrespectful ones in our family. Not only that I put them in their place, but also, I put them out of my house. I didn't care about anything they said.

Janice:

Do any of the family members talk to you now or are they talking to you at all?

Mildred:

Unfortunately, three of them passed away before we were able to put everything behind us. There are a couple of family members that we have that we have put our differences behind us. Some don't even bother to open up after I have tried reaching out to them.

<u>Janice:</u>

Grandma, that is sad. Family is definitely important. I am truly appreciating what I have right in front of me. I promise I will never take it for granted again. You have never shown any signs of what I would consider a lot of hurt and pain.

<u>Mildred:</u>

A lot of times, you have to mask something that is really hurtful to protect those who may never understand. I prayed about it and did everything within my power to make sure that everything was right and that we all were on the same page. It was always a fight and a struggle. The most hurting feeling was looking my family right in the face and they know that I was hurting and done nothing about it. I thought that I would develop hatred but I didn't. I could not bring myself to their level. I knew when it came to taking care of my own family, I had to rise and be better than the environment that I am a product of. In the midst of being very unhappy, I had to hide it at all cost to protect the interest of my family. I could not allow them to start off unhappy when I know that there is opportunity for happiness. Keep that near and dear to your heart and you should not have any problems. You get you some rest so you will not be tired at your appointment tomorrow.

<u>Janice:</u>

You have a good night Grandma. You definitely said a mouthful.

"EVERYONE CALLS IT A NIGHT"

"THE NEXT MORNING AT THE COUNSELOR'S OFFICE"

Cheryl:

Good morning to the both of you. How is everything going?

Janice:

I would have to say that everything is coming along just great. I feel that we have made some progress towards our goal.

Cheryl:

De'Andre, do you agree with what she is saying?

De'Andre:

I do. One thing that I can say is that we seem to be communicating a little more plus I feel in a lot of ways that I am being heard more than I ever been. The last few conversations we have had didn't lead into an argument.

Cheryl:

That is great. The communication piece is very important because you would need to be able to talk in order to work out problems. Janice in any way, do you feel any insecurities when it comes to De'Andre?

Janice:

I feel that the insecurities were just obstacles that I have to work on. I would also say it would probably be my hormones as well. I am not going to lie, before De'Andre I was hurt a few times. I think I carried a little bit of that with me throughout my life. It was just a part of me that I had never let go. It is hard especially when it was something that you became use to. I do know that De'Andre did absorb and suffered from my past events of bad experiences. I am truly sorry for putting him through that.

Cheryl:

The important thing is that you acknowledge your flaws and making progress to move forward. That is truly a commendable because people have been known to make excuses. It only proves that you are trying to salvage everything that is obviously important. De'Andre, can you accept what she is proclaiming?

De'Andre:

I absolutely can. I look at us and think about how long we have been married, it is worth sustaining. I look at both of my daughters and smile about having a beautiful family. I would not trade it for anything in the world. I don't expect perfection because I know that we are not perfect. Being committed and having an understanding of each other is very important. Taking those vows meant that and then some.

Cheryl:

To me, it seems like things are working out for the both of you. I am feeling a sense of happiness between you two. I will definitely recommend one thing. I know that the both of you are hardworking people. At least once a month, make time for each other. Go back down memory lane to the time you two started dating.

De'Andre:

I love the idea.

Janice:

That is a great idea to me as well.

De'Andre:

We can turn that into an event since our wedding anniversary is approaching. We are coming up on twenty-eight years and still counting.

Cheryl:

That is a great start. Twenty-eight years of marital bliss. That is something to be truly thankful for. Well, we can end this session. I don't really think we need to schedule another session unless you feel that it is necessary. I feel that you two are on the right track for success. You can always give me a call if it is deemed necessary.

Janice:

Ok great. You take care and thank you so much.

De'Andre:

Thank you Cheryl. Greatly appreciate it.

END OF SCENE 7

SCENE 8 – FOREVER LOVE AND HAPPINESS:

"GATHERING FOR THE ANNIVERSARY EVENT"

Mildred:

Janice, we are about to have a house full for the anniversary party. You are about to celebrate twenty-eight years of marital bliss. You are embarking up on a milestone because in most cases, people are not staying married that long. What you have is definitely worth appreciating and preserving.

Janice:

I have to agree with you Grandma. I want to take this moment to thank you for everything that you have done. You have always given me great advice and you supported me like no other. You helped me stay focused on what is the most important. You supported my marriage throughout anything. You also never tried taking advantage of me. Along with my daughters, you have been one of my biggest cheerleaders. I always felt love when it comes to you. No one else in the family comes close to matching that.

Mildred:

My mother taught me the value of what family is suppose to be. I Grew up in an environment where we knew how to love each other. My parents did not allow conflict in the house because that can lead to carrying out problems outside of the home. When I met your grandfather, it was easy for me to share and experience unconditional love because we vowed to each other to not allow any outside distractions. I am not saying that we were perfect, but in my heart, we had a perfect marriage. We got on each other's nerves but we never wanted out of the marriage. It was until death do us part and I would not look back and trade it for anything. He was the love of my life. That is the reason that I am so adamant when it comes to you and De'Andre. I know you are the love of his life. I see the way that he looks at you with love written all over his face. When you have that, hold on to that because it is a very rare breed.

Janice:

Well said Grandma. That is why I always take advice from you. I am not only going to get the truth out of you, but everything you say makes perfect sense. I see people are starting to roll up. Hey everyone. Glad that you can make it.

Sherise, Malaysha & Jermaine:

Hey there Janice.

Janice:

Give me your coats so I can put them in the room. Finger foods are in the dining room.

Jermaine:

Let me make my way to the dining room because I haven't eaten all day.

Malaysha:

Girl, everything looks nice. You all did a very nice job decorating. I love the personalized napkins.

Janice:

Thank you. My grandmother got those made for me.

Sherise:

That was really sweet of her. I am going to ask her where she got them made at. I have a cousin that will be getting married in the next six to nine months and I know that she would love this.

Janice:

I know where she got them from. It is a store that does monogramming located in the shopping enter a couple of blocks from where we work. That store gets a lot of business.

<u>Sherise:</u>

I am going to check that out. Who is that walking?

<u>Janice:</u>

That is both of my sisters. Hey there you two.

<u>Myesha & Rhonda:</u>

Hey there sis.

<u>Janice:</u>

I know what you two are looking for. It is in the dining room (lol).

<u>Myesha:</u>

I need something on my stomach.

<u>Janice:</u>

Anyone of you heard from Dominic?

<u>Rhonda:</u>

He said that he will be here in a bit. He had some place to stop at before he made it here.

<u>Myesha:</u>

Janice, everything looks very nice. Just to think, you two have been married for twenty-eight years. It really seems like it was only yesterday.

<u>Janice:</u>

These years have flown by. Rhonda, open the door. Here comes Felicia and Tianna.

<u>Felicia & Tianna:</u>

Hey, how is everyone?

<u>Janice:</u>

Everything is good. Glad you two can make it.

Myesha:

Felicia, love that hairstyle. I need to make my way by your shop. I am long overdue.

Felicia:

I am off Friday but if you are available, I will come in for you.

Myesha:

I will take you up on your offer. I will be leaving town Saturday morning for a week.

Felicia:

Ok cool. Meet me in the morning when we open.

Myesha:

That will definitely work. I will still be able to get some things done while it is still early.

Tianna:

Janice, does the twenty-eight years of marriage feel surreal?

Janice:

It is a great feeling knowing you have someone that can love you unconditionally for so long. I never thought it would happen for me. After the prior bad experiences, I just never gave my hopes up on it happening.

Tianna:

I am proud of the both of you because nowadays you do not see marriages last that long. You give inspiration and hope for a successful marriage. I can say that I have not given up any hope. There was one guy that I thought was the one but it wasn't meant to be for us.

Felicia:

I totally agree with you Tianna. Janice and De'Andre have set the bar. The guy you thought that was for you, God just let you know that he was only here for a season.

Mildred:

Dominic is coming up the walkway.

Dominic:

Hey Grandma. Hello everyone. Sis, I want to take this moment to say congratulations on twenty-eight years of marriage. I also want to take this moment to apologize to you for so much grief that I have caused you. It is no secret of what I did but I want you to know that I mean it from the bottom of my heart. You did not deserve any of it. I have been talking to some counselors at the community center that has been helping me with my issues. For the most part, things are really working for me.

Janice:

Dominic, that is great. I am glad that things are working out for you. I accept your apology as well. I know that you have been going through a rough patch but at least you are getting the help that you need.

De'Andre:

Hey everyone. Miguel and Syerra, you know Mrs. Mildred and Janice's sisters and brothers. These are Janice co-workers Sherise, Malaysha and Jermaine. These are Janice's childhood friends Felicia and Tianna.

Miguel & Syerra:

It's very nice to meet you all.

Felicia:

I know you. You are a fitness instructor at the gym around the corner from my shop I work in. One of my clients highly recommends you.

<u>Syerra:</u>

That is definitely great to know. I have a couple of business cards for you. My objective is to help people reach their goals.

<u>Felicia:</u>

You can expect me to start coming to your class. I need to get right. I have been procrastinating long enough. No more of the new year's resolution.

<u>Syerra:</u>

Girl, I got you. Let me open this door. De'Andre, your co-worker just pulled up.

<u>Kandace:</u>

Hello everyone. Where is that good smelling food (lol).

<u>Yolanda:</u>

It is in the other room. Wait until you see the cake that we got my mom and dad.

<u>Kandace:</u>

You all were able to accomplish it without him finding out? You all got it pass the mystery solver (lol).

<u>Yolanda:</u>

Trust me, it wasn't easy. We sent my mom out for a pampering session and she still doesn't inside the house.

<u>Belinda:</u>

Someone is walking up the walkway. It's Carmen and Danielle. Hey there cousins.

Carmen & Danielle:

Hey cousin. Point us in the direction of the food (lol).

Yolanda:

Belinda, were you able to get in touch with Lachelle?

Belinda:

I was able to get her after three tries but I will not get my hopes up on her showing up. You know how Lachelle is. She will appear out of nowhere and before you know it, she is giving you a story when it comes to her kids.

Yolanda:

She probably didn't have anyone to watch her kids. You know that she is pretty much doing this solo.

Belinda:

So true. I am about to grab something to eat before everything get started. I love how we got everything set up for everyone to say they part and the impact and memories that they all have with them.

Mildred:

Yolanda, you about ready to get started? I will have to say that you and Belinda have outdid yourselves getting everything decorated and set up. I know that this is going to be an anniversary that both of them will always remember and never forget.

Yolanda:

Yes indeed Grandma. Everyone is about finish with their finger foods. I am going to have Belinda grab the cake and roll it out. I am so glad that the table has wheels.

Mildred:

Ok. I will start having people gather in the living room.

Yolanda:

Belinda, Grandma is having everyone gather into the living room. I want you to roll the cake into the living room.

Belinda:

Who is that getting dropped off?

Yolanda:

That is Lachelle. Let me go and run a little interference before she comes into the house and start running her mouth prematurely.

Belinda:

Good idea.

Yolanda:

Hey Lachelle, glad that you were able to make it. Where are the kids?

Lachelle:

They are with their grandmothers. They will be with them for the next couple of days which gives me a little break. I am really glad that I was able to make it. I owe your mom an apology. I know that I have caused her a lot of heartache.

Yolanda:

I would wait until you two are alone. I think she will be happy knowing that you showed up.

Lachelle:

Ok cousin, I will wait. As long as she is happy, I want to make sure that I keep it that way. I am not here to spoil anyone's moment especially for this event for her and De'Andre.

Yolanda:

As a matter of fact, here she comes.

Janice:

Hey Lachelle, I am glad that you were able to make it.

Lachelle:

Girl, this is you and De'Andre's special day and I did not want to miss it. First, I want to start off by saying congratulations to the both of you on twenty-eight years of marriage. That is truly a blessing. I also wanted share that I am jealous of you because you found your Knight in Shining Armor. Most important, I do want to apologize for the things that I have did and the awkward positions that I got you mixed up in. I said to myself that I know that your husband doesn't care for me at all. The one thing that I can say is that I have never gotten a negative vibe from him.

Janice:

Lachelle trust me, if he didn't care for you, he would have rushed you out of the house quicker than you came in. He seen when you arrived so if there was an issue you would not have made it pass the front door. Let's consider what happened as water under the bridge.

Lachelle:

Thank you cousin. I am glad that you didn't give up and stop talking to me. My struggle has been very rough but it is about to turn around. The courts got involved and now those deadbeat dads of my kids are getting ready to be forced to pay child support.

Janice:

That is good. It is their responsibility anyway.

Yolanda:

Good afternoon everyone. Can I have everybody's attention for a second? We want to take this time to thank everyone for coming out to help celebrate my mom and dad's wedding anniversary. Twenty-eight years of marriage is definitely a milestone. The way I see it, my parents have set the bar for me and my sister to one day follow. They exemplify to us what we would consider an ideal marriage. With that being said, we want to have both of you sit in these chairs we have reserved right here in front of the mantle. We are going to have everyone come up and say something from their perspective what impact you two have been on them. First, I want to have Belinda bring out your surprise.

Belinda:

Especially for the both you, this cake was designed with a lot of thought in mind. The color scheme was compliments of Grandma. She told us the color you two wore when the both of you first met.

Yolanda:

As you can see, those colors still stuck with you two till this day.

Janice:

That is truly a beautiful cake. That is a very unique design.

De'Andre:

That is very unique. I have never seen a cake designated with such detail. You two knocked that out of the park. Thank you both.

Yolanda & Belinda:

You are welcome.

Mildred:

That is very nice.

Yolanda:

I will start slicing the cake while people are coming to the podium to speak on their segment to our guests of honor. First person that we would like to call up is our grandmother, the matriarch of the family.

<u>Mildred:</u>

I want to say thank you all again for coming out to celebrate this illustrious occasion. Twenty-eight years of marriage is truly a blessing. I want to take this moment to say that I love you both and admire the love you share between the two of you. I am thankful for the both of you. The both of you openly welcomed me into your home and I am truly thankful for that. Many blessings to you two on this special day.

<u>Yolanda:</u>

Next, my aunt Syerra and my uncle Miguel.

<u>Syerra:</u>

Greetings to everyone. I will not make a long speech. I want to say that I am truly happy for the both of you. Twenty-eight years of marital bliss. God bless you both.

<u>Miguel:</u>

My brother has always been an inspiration to me. His success has showed me that you can do anything that you put your mind too. When he first told me about Janice, I said to myself that this must be an outstanding woman to win my brother's heart. Twenty-eight years of marriage has proven to me how outstanding she really is. I want to thank you for making my brother the happiest man in the world. It brings my heart joy. I love you both and may God continue to bless this union.

<u>Yolanda:</u>

Thank you Aunt Syerra and Uncle Miguel. Next up is my aunts Myesha & Rhonda and Uncle Dominic.

Myesha:

Greetings everyone. Growing up with my siblings, I can say was very exciting. Janice was our guide in life because she made sure that everything was all good. Being the oldest, we all looked up to her. She always gave the best advice. When De'Andre came into her life, I thought there would be a disconnect because now she is with someone. I was wrong. In fact, De'Andre came to us with open arms as if we were his younger siblings. A match made in heaven and I am glad that Janice got to marry her best friend. Congratulations to the both of you and God bless.

Rhonda:

How can I follow behind Myesha's speech (lol)? She covered a lot of the vital portions of Janice and the impact she created. When De'Andre came along, they became a dynamic duo. I am truly happy to be a part of a celebration highlighting two beautiful souls that means the world to me. I want to say Happy Anniversary and I Love you both.

Dominic:

I want to start off by saying congratulations to the both of you on a long prosperous marriage. I have never been a person of many words. Today, I have to acknowledge two individuals that has made a major impact. My sister Janice has put up with a lot when it came to me. I know that I am not perfect but I am gracefully humble that she never gave up on me. I also want to thank De'Andre for not giving up on me as well. He is definitely the big brother I always wished of having. Truly a great guy that gave good advice and never sugarcoated anything. I love you both and many marital blessings in the future to come.

Yolanda:

Next, I want to call up our cousins Danielle, Carmen and Lachelle.

Danielle:

Congratulations to the both of you. I am so happy for you two. Seeing my cousin Janice happy warms my heart. When we were young, we use to say that one day we will find the ideal man that will become our husband and have a family. Twenty-eight years of marital bliss just proves that dreams do come true. You two were definitely made for each other. Love you both and may God continue to bless you abundantly.

Carmen:

Hello everyone. I want to say congratulations to Janice and De'Andre on their wedding anniversary. These two are definitely a match made in heaven just as Myesha said. Twenty-eight years of marriage is a major milestone that I look at as total success. Janice and De'Andre have always encouraged me when it came to starting a business. Because of them, I own my own business as of today. I want to thank the both of you for the consistent encouragement and support. Congratulations again and I love you both.

Lachelle:

Greetings everyone. I want to say Happy Anniversary to my favorite couple. I am honored to be a part of this celebration. Janice has been an inspiration to me ever since I was a little girl. She was and still is my big sister figure. She has a heart of gold. Celebrating this special occasion with Janice and De'Andre is truly a blessing to me. I love you both and wish you many more marital blessings to come.

Yolanda:

Thank you Lachelle. Next, I want to introduce my dad's co-worker and business partner Kandace.

Kandace:

Thank you Yolanda. Hello beautiful family. I want to take this moment to congratulate Janice and De'Andre of twenty-eight years of marriage. It is not that often that you find it, but when you do, it is definitely a beautiful thing. I have been De'Andre's co-worker and now business partner for over twenty years. He has taught me a great deal about the business in which I am truly grateful for. He would talk about Janice and his daughters as if someone was telling me a fairytale. There was always this glow about him that took him to his happy place when he would talk about her. When I met Janice, I totally understood why he was so happy. She is a beautiful individual inside and outside. The love that these two shares is priceless. She has helped me by sharing great advice about business ventures. My favorite was when she told me to reach for the stars because one day, I will be able to grab one. When I look at Janice and De'Andre, I look at a couple who has all the stars and the kind of people they are, they would share the stars with us. The opportunity of going into business was what I considered a star that I received from De'Andre. De'Andre being the mentor, he has taught me so much about the business, he felt very confident in me going into business with him. He was very clear that it was up to me to reach for that star. The support that his family gave, I could not pass it up. Janice and De'Andre motivated me to become what I am today. Again, I want to say congratulations on your special day and I thank you both on your continuing support. Thank you for being the star that was destined for me to reach. I love you both and God bless this union.

<u>Yolanda:</u>

Thank you Kandace. Now I want to call up my mother's childhood friends Tianna and Felicia. They have been friends since the beginning of elementary.

<u>Tianna:</u>

Major congratulations to the both of you on twenty-eight years of marriage. I am so glad to see my childhood friend live her dream. When we were young, we would sit up and talk all night about everything. She was always my big sister to turn to. She always encouraged me to follow my dream. I really never knew what I wanted to do until going to work with my aunt and uncle one day to help them file and organize paperwork. I was doing it part time at their dentist office for a little while. After witnessing a couple of routine visits and not being the one in the chair, I found it very interesting. I shared what I felt to Janice and helped me research some schools to attend. Janice and my mother were my two biggest cheerleaders. Because of that, I am a dentist today. She married her best friend which became the big brother that I never had. Definitely a beautiful couple indeed and I wish them both the best. Love you guys.

<u>Felicia:</u>

I want to take this brief moment to say Happy Anniversary to two individuals that I love dearly. I am kind of piggy-backing off of what Tianna was saying when it comes to following dreams. I first started doing hair in high school in which Janice was the first one that took a chance on me (lol). She said I seen the good job that you did with your doll's hair and now it is time to try it on a real person. Of course, I did not use the chemicals that we use today. The only thing that I had was a couple of curling irons, a hair dryer and everyone's go to, that green hair grease (lol). That was my start off and Janice was my model. I did a variety of hairstyles that I took pictures of Janice wearing so I could show to others. One day, Janice told me to quit playing, get your license and whatever certification and open you a salon. During that time, I was in school for cosmetology. She said as soon as you finish, work a little under someone whose been around a long time then plan on opening your own salon shortly afterwards. I said, how long is shortly? She said realistically within three years but shoot for six months. I said to myself, six months would be impossible. Janice never let me feel that anything is impossible. In exactly fifteen months, I became the owner of my own beauty salon. Janice always told me that I would grab the star that I reached for before I knew it. I want to thank my childhood friend for the continuing encouraging words. Again, Happy Anniversary and congratulations on twenty-eight years. Many blessings to you both.

Yolanda:

Now, I want to bring up my mother's co-workers Jermaine, Sherise and Malaysha.

Jermaine:

Greetings everyone. I am not a man of very many words but I would like to say congratulations to Janice and De'Andre on their wedding anniversary. Janice taught me quite much about my job. I started off as an intern under her tutelage. As of last week, it marks twelve years that I have been working with Janice. It is the best job I have ever had and would not trade it for anything. I thank you for being my mentor. I also thank De'Andre for the great advice he has given me. God bless you both.

Sherise:

Greetings everyone. Happy Anniversary to this beautiful couple. I have to basically piggy-back on what Jermaine said. I was also an intern before becoming a permanent employee in which I am at fourteen years in. Both Janice and De'Andre have always given me great advice. I am truly thankful for the impact that they have had on me. God bless you both.

Malaysha:

Greetings all. I want to start off by wishing Janice and De'Andre a Happy Anniversary. This is truly a blessing that you hardly see anymore. I remember it like it was yesterday when I started working with Janice. She immediately welcomed me with open arms. I had just graduated from college and relocated to branch off for a different experience. Janice also helped me find my first home after living in an apartment that I found online (vow to never do that again). It was such a relief. Just to think, it has been twenty years that I have been working with Janice. She is such an inspiration to me. She is always thinking positive and she is very upbeat. When I first met De'Andre, I was fascinated with the way he treated her and how thoughtful he was. He would send flowers just because. Every so often, he would have lunch delivered to all of us. He is truly a caring and giving person. I see both of them as the perfect match. Again, to the both of you, I want to say Happy Anniversary. May God continue to bless you with many more.

Yolanda:

Thank you Malaysha. Now last but not least, me and my sister would like to share our story before both guests of honor come to the podium. First, I would like to say Happy Anniversary and I love you both. You two have loved me and my sister unconditionally and we are forever thankful for that. You have taught us so much about taking ownership and responsibility of our own destiny no matter what it is. You have also taught me the concept of independence. I could not ask for better parents. God has truly blessed me. I love you two dearly.

Belinda:

My sister stole all the thunder (lol). I want to wish my mom and dad a Happy Anniversary. It warms my heart to see after twenty-eight that they are still in love like they just met. That is truly inspirational to me. They both have taught me so many life lessons that has been very beneficial to me. They have been a great support system since day one. I do not have enough time to explain why they are the best parents in the world, but I know that I wouldn't trade it for anything in the world. To me, they are the prime example of dreams coming true. I love you both dearly and now it is time for me to step aside so you two to come share your story.

Yolanda:

Thank you Sis. I want to thank everyone for their kind words. Now, it is time for the reason why we are here today. I bring up our guests of honor, my mother Mrs. Janice Jones and my father Mr. De'Andre Jones.

"APPLAUSING"

Janice:

Oh my God, thank you so much. Thank you all. Man, I have to start off by saying "God is good all the time, and all the time God is good". Beautiful words spoken by everyone. I truly appreciate it. I am overwhelmed with happiness right now and I do not know where to start. I look around the room and I can say that I am receiving so much love in return that I give on a daily basis. Thank you from the bottom of my heart. I definitely have to say that dreams do come true. When I was a little girl, I use to say that when I get older, I am going to college to get my education, get married and have kids. I was able to accomplish that and then some with my soulmate De'Andre. I have a quick story on how we met. I was at the store with my mom. I was walking down the aisle pushing a cart not really paying attention. As I was turning the corner, I ran into some items that fell into his cart. Of course, I apologized but he told me that I can help him put everything back or I can give him my number. We exchanged numbers and I departed the store. My mom asked if I was going to call. I said that I do not know. This young man could be your future. Just to think, we are here celebrating twenty-eight years of marriage. I would do this all over again. The funny thing is once a year, we go back to that same store where we first met. We honor that day as the very beginning of us. We go to that very same aisle and share a kiss. Those are the moments that are so special because it is the little things that creates the best memories. I am going to take this whole month to celebrate our anniversary because after twenty-eight years, there is not enough time in one day to squeeze everything in. Again, I want to thank everyone for coming out to help me and De'Andre celebrate our special day. We greatly appreciate everyone that has been a part in our lives. Now, I will turn it over to my one and only, my best friend and husband De'Andre.

"APPLAUSING"

De'Andre:

Greetings all. God is good. He is my source of strength. He has said it in his word. Philippians 4:13, I can do all things through Christ who strengthens me. Adding God into everything that you do, you can never go wrong. We went before God and took vows, and here we are celebrating twenty-eight years of our marital bliss. I thank him every day for bringing Janice into my life. I have so many memories that I can share but I know we would not have enough time for everything. I will hit on a couple of key memories that I could say that was very impactful to me. Before we officially met in the store where we exchanged phone numbers, I saw Janice a couple of times in passing around the neighborhood. The first time I saw Janice, she was at the park with some friends playing a little old school music. I made my way over to say hello. Her reply hello, how are doing? The next time I saw her was at a carnival that came to town. I made my way to speak and this time I was like hey gorgeous. Her reply was he there handsome, nice to see you again. I said to her, same here. We went on our way and I went to get something to eat. I knew right then that I had to have her. I said to myself, if I see her again, we will exchange information and be together. Here we are running into each other in the grocery store. I was a little nervous at first because her mother was with her. Since I was determined to get her, I had to make sure that I was on my best behavior. When I approached her for her number after she knocked some items in my cart (lol), she laughed at first then gave me her number. Her mom's first words were so you are going to be my daughter's future husband? I said yes ma'am I am and I promise that I would take good care of her. Another funny part to the story is lasagna is my favorite meal. The significance of the store visit was when she ran into my cart which pushed it into the shelf, there were lasagna noodles that fell into my cart (lol). We go back to that same spot in that store every year where we relive that moment. I am surprised that the store hasn't been changed around after all these years. It is the little things that means a lot. When I look back at what started everything, those are the memories that are the most priceless. I want to take this moment to wish my soulmate a Happy Anniversary. You brought so much joy into my life. I thank you dearly for everything. I also want to thank everyone for coming out to our anniversary celebration. I truly appreciate it.

END OF SCENE 8

SUMMARIZATION:

From the author's perspective, when we have a family, we take on a great deal of responsibilities. The range of that responsibility is a very broad one. Sometimes we may not know what we are taking on until later down the line. There are a couple of differences when we talk about taking on the responsibility of a family. We have immediate family and we have extended family. Now we ask ourselves, what correlation does one have with the other. That is where we would bridge the gap when it comes to the responsibility part. When two individuals get married, they become an immediate family. Everyone else that you are related to becomes the extended family. In some cases, it creates a problem that really neither of the individuals who got married are so much at fault. As time goes on throughout a marriage, the responsibility of each individuals determines if they will become part of a problem or part of a solution. In a marriage, being devoted to each other is extremely important. When a couple gets married, they become one cohesive unit. We run into problems that would eventually become major when you have those that refuse to accept the fact that they have became the extended family of someone they have known as their relative all of their lives. Those of the extended family develop their own selfish perspective feeling that their family member should just agree with them regardless of the lack of respect they have for the one that their relative have committed to. Us as individuals who have commitments to others have full control of their reaction towards those who are outside of your immediate responsibility. When we make irrational decisions, the commitment becomes compromised. When we are willing to do that, then we are willingly destroying the unification between two into one. You have to make the decision that is in aligned with your commitment. Once that is done, the unification is in total happiness. Remember, your promise is to God and the individual that you are committed to.

Made in the USA
Columbia, SC
26 December 2023

29493400R00126